Marilyn Taylor's

muffin
madness

Marilyn Taylor's
muffin madness

Quick and Healthy Recipes for Today's Busy Lifestyles

Rhodes & Easton
Traverse City, Michigan

Published by Rhodes &Easton
121 E. Front St., Traverse City, Michigan 49684

Publisher's Cataloging-in-Publication Data
Taylor, Marilyn.
    Muffin madness: quick and healthy recipes for today's busy lifestyles / Marilyn Taylor.—Traverse City, MI:
    Rhodes & Easton Publishing, c1997.
        p.   ill.   cm.
    Includes index.
    ISBN: 0-9649401-0-8
    1. Muffins.   2. Low-fat diet—recipes.
    3. Cookery.   I. Title.
    TX770.M83 T39   1997
    641.815 dc—21   96-72268

PROJECT COORDINATED BY JENKINS GROUP, INC.

00   99   98   ❖   5   4   3   2   1

Printed in the United States of America

This book is dedicated to Mary Tomasi, my grandmother.

Grandma, I can still remember the smell of fresh baked "gramala" bread coming from your kitchen and it fills me with many happy memories.

Contents

Contents

Preface

As a former t.v. talk show host and producer, I had more than ample opportunities to be creative on a daily basis. Enter motherhood. The new challenge became how to use my creative energies and still be at home for my two small children.

For years I had been accumulating an extensive collection of great muffin recipes. So when a friend suggested I share these recipes with others, it was an answer to my prayer.

I decided to compile my favorite muffin recipes into book form. They range from the simple to the more substantive. I also learned the value of the old adage, "Bloom where you are planted."

Acknowledgments

I thank the Lord who has proven to me that in all things God works for the good of those who love him.

Also, I thank my parents, George and Bettey Tomasi, from whom I inherited my love for learning. They are truly an inspiration. And, I thank my husband Tom, and children Paul and Gina who gave me the two most important ingredients that went into writing this book — love and encouragement.

Apple Muffins

2 cups whole wheat flour
1 tbsp. baking powder
1 tsp. cinnamon
2 egg whites or 1 egg

³/₄ cup milk
¹/₄ cup honey
¹/₄ cup oil
1 cup apple, peeled
and chopped

Mix dry ingredients. Combine egg, milk, honey, oil, and apples; mix well. Add wet ingredients to dry ingredients, stir. Bake at 375 degrees for 20 minutes.

Apple, Cinnamon, and Raisin Muffins

2 cups flour
1 tbsp. baking powder
¹/₂ tsp. nutmeg
²/₃ cup apple juice

¹/₃ cup oil
1 apple, grated
1 tsp. cinnamon
¹/₂ cup raisins

Combine all ingredients. Bake at 400 degrees for 15 to 20 minutes.

SERVING SUGGESTION: Make Cinnamon Crumble Topping – Mix 4 tbsp. sugar, 2 tbsp. flour, 1/2 tsp. cinnamon, and 1 tbsp. softened butter. Mix well by rubbing together with fingers. Sprinkle on muffin tops before baking.

Apple Carrot Muffins

In a large bowl add and combine well:

3 eggs

$^2/_3$ cup sugar

$^1/_2$ cup vegetable oil

$1^1/_4$ cups shredded apple

1 cup shredded carrots

$1^1/_4$ tsp. vanilla

In smaller bowl combine well:

1 cup graham flour

1 cup cake flour

1 tbsp. baking powder

$^1/_2$ tsp. baking soda

$^1/_4$ tsp. salt

$^3/_4$ tsp. ground cinnamon

$^1/_2$ cup chopped walnuts
    (optional)

Combine wet and dry mixtures and fold together gently, until just mixed. Spoon into prepared muffin tins and decorate top of each muffin with a walnut. Bake at 375 degrees for 25 to 30 minutes. Remove from pan and cool on rack.

Hint: Toss shredded apple in lemon juice. Apple slices will stay fresh looking longer.

Double Apple Muffins

1¹/₂ cups flour
1 cup oatmeal
¹/₃ cup firmly packed
    brown sugar
1 tbsp. baking powder
1 tsp. cinnamon

¹/₂ tsp. salt
²/₃ cup milk
¹/₃ cup apple juice
¹/₄ cup vegetable oil
1 egg, beaten
³/₄ apple, peeled
    and chopped

Preheat oven to 400 degrees. Line 12 muffin tins with baking papers. Combine dry ingredients. Combine remaining ingredients. Stir together. Fill muffin tins 2/3 full. Bake 20 to 22 minutes. Makes 12 muffins at 160 calories each.

Apricot Almond Muffins

2 cups flour
3 tsp. baking powder
¹/₂ tsp. salt
2 tbsp. sugar
1 egg, lightly beaten
1 cup milk

¹/₄ cup butter or
    margarine, melted
¹/₂ cup dried
    apricots, chopped
¹/₂ cup slivered almonds

Preheat oven to 350 degrees. Line muffin tins with paper. Mix dry ingredients. Add the egg, milk, and butter; stirring only enough to moisten the flour mixture. Fill muffin tins 2/3 full. Bake for 20 to 25 minutes.

Applesauce Muffins

Very soft and spicy with applesauce and raisins.

1 large egg	³/₄ tsp. baking soda
2 tbsp. vegetable oil	2 tsp. baking powder
1¹/₂ cups unsweetened	¹/₂ tsp. nutmeg
applesauce	¹/₂ tsp. cinnamon
2 cups flour	³/₄ cup raisins

Topping:

1-8 oz. package cream	milk
cheese, softened	

Beat together egg, oil, and applesauce. Add flour, baking soda, baking powder, and spices; beat well. Stir in raisins. Spoon batter into oiled and floured muffin wells. Bake at 375 degrees for 20 to 25 minutes or until firm to the touch and browned. Cool on wire racks.

TO MAKE TOPPING, cream together cream cheese and just enough milk to make a thick, spreadable mixture. Spread over cooled muffins and serve. Serves 12.

 Americans eat approximately 22 pounds of apples per year per person.

Apricot Ginger Muffins

Delicious for breakfast, these muffins are also good with lunch or afternoon tea.

1³/₄ cups sifted flour
4 tbsp. sugar
2¹/₂ tsp. baking powder
1¹/₂ tsp. ground ginger
¹/₄ tsp. salt
1 egg

³/₄ cup milk
¹/₃ cup butter or margarine,
   melted
³/₄ cup dried apricots,
   finely cut-up
1¹/₄ tsp. grated fresh lemon
   rind (1 lemon)

Preheat oven to 400 degrees. Grease the bottoms only of twelve muffin tins. Sift together the flour, sugar, baking powder, ginger, and salt into a large bowl. Lightly beat the egg in a small bowl. Beat in the milk and butter; stir in the apricots and lemon rind. Pour all at once into the flour mixture. Stir briskly with a fork, just until all the ingredients are just moistened. The batter will look lumpy. Fill muffin tins 2/3 full. Bake in the preheated oven for 25 minutes or until golden brown. Remove muffins from pan at once. Garnish with additional cut-up dried apricots, if you desire. Serve piping hot.

Hint: To remove hard brown sugar from a box, just add a few drops of water to the box and microwave on high for a few seconds.

Banana Muffins

1¹/₂ cups flour
¹/₂ cup sugar
2 tsp. baking powder
¹/₂ tsp. salt

1 egg, lightly beaten
¹/₂ cup milk
¹/₄ cup vegetable oil
³/₄ cup mashed ripe banana

Combine flour, sugar, baking powder, and salt in large bowl. In smaller bowl combine egg, milk, oil, and banana; stir just until flour mixture is moistened. Fill muffin tins 2/3 full. Bake at 400 degrees for 20 to 25 minutes. Yield: 16 muffins.

Banana Orange Muffins

1¹/₂ cups flour
1 cup oatmeal
¹/₃ cup firmly packed
    brown sugar
1 tbsp. baking powder
¹/₂ tsp. baking soda

¹/₄ tsp. salt
²/₃ cup mashed ripe banana
¹/₂ cup orange juice
1 egg, lightly beaten
¹/₂ tsp. grated orange peel

Preheat oven to 400 degrees. Line muffin tins. Combine dry ingredients in large bowl. In smaller bowl combine remaining ingredients, add to flour mixture. Pour into muffin tins. Bake 20 minutes or until golden brown. Makes 12 muffins at 190 calories each.

Banana Raisin Muffins

2 cups whole wheat flour
1 cup unprocessed bran flakes
1 cup rolled oats
1¹/₂ tsp. baking soda
2 egg whites

³/₄ cup frozen apple juice, thawed
¹/₂ cup plain lowfat yogurt
1 cup mashed bananas
1 cup raisins

Combine the flour, bran flakes, rolled oats, and baking soda in a large bowl. Beat the egg whites in a small bowl until stiff peaks form. Set aside. Add the apple juice, yogurt, bananas, and raisins to the flour mixture; stir to blend. Fold in the egg whites; mix well. Spoon the batter into paper-lined muffin tins. Bake at 400 degrees for 20 minutes.

Banana Walnut Muffins

1¹/₃ cups flour
¹/₄ tsp. salt
1 tsp. baking soda
³/₄ tsp. baking powder

²/₃ cup sugar
1 tsp. lemon juice
6 tbsp. margarine, softened
2 bananas, mashed

Mix dry ingredients. Mash bananas, add softened margarine, lemon juice, and sugar. Add mixture to dry ingredients; mix well. Bake at 350 degrees for 25 minutes.

Healthy Blueberry Muffins

1 cup blueberries
$^1/_4$ cup whole wheat flour
1 cup whole wheat flour
$1^3/_4$ tsp. baking powder
$^1/_2$ tsp. salt
$^1/_2$ tsp. cinnamon

$^1/_2$ cup wheat germ
3 tbsp. oil
$^1/_4$ cup brown sugar
1 egg, lightly beaten
$^3/_4$ cup milk

Preheat oven to 375 degrees. Prepare a 12 cup muffin tin. Wash and drain the berries; sprinkle with the 1/4 cup flour and let them sit while you prepare the batter. Sift together the remaining flour, baking powder, salt, and cinnamon. Add the wheat germ. Cream the oil, sugar, and egg. Add the milk and dry ingredients, stirring just enough to mix. Fold in the blueberries. Spoon into muffin tins, filling nearly full. Bake for 15 to 20 minutes.

Cherry Banana Muffins

$1^3/_4$ cups flour
2 tsp. baking powder
$^1/_4$ tsp. baking soda
$^1/_8$ tsp. salt
$^1/_3$ cup shortening

$^2/_3$ cup sugar
2 eggs, lightly beaten
$^2/_3$ cup mashed ripe banana
$1^1/_4$ cups sliced
    maraschino cherries

Sift together flour, baking powder, baking soda, and salt. Cream shortening. Gradually add sugar; beat until light and fluffy. Add eggs; mix well. Add dry ingredients alternately with bananas. Fold in cherries. Spoon into prepared muffin tins. Bake at 350 degrees for 30 to 35 minutes.

Michigan's Best Cherry Muffins

1 cup flour
$^{3}/_{4}$ cup oat bran
$^{2}/_{3}$ cup sugar
1 tbsp. baking powder
$^{1}/_{4}$ tsp. salt
$^{3}/_{4}$ cup skim milk
$^{1}/_{2}$ cup nonfat yogurt

$^{1}/_{3}$ cup margarine,
   melted and cooled
2 egg whites, lightly beaten
1 tsp. vanilla extract
1 cup dried cherries
$^{1}/_{2}$ cup chopped walnuts
$1^{1}/_{2}$ tsp. grated orange peel

In a medium bowl combine flour, oat bran, sugar, baking powder, and salt. Mix well. In another mixing bowl combine milk, yogurt, melted margarine, egg whites, and vanilla extract. Stir milk mixture into flour mixture. Mix just until ingredients are moistened. Fold cherries, walnuts, and orange peel into batter. Spoon batter into prepared muffin tins. Bake in preheated 400 degree oven for 20 to 25 minutes. Yield: 12 to 15 muffins.

Traverse City, Michigan is the cherry capital of the world. There are more than two million cherry trees in the Grand Traverse region.

Cherry Orange Muffins

1 cup sugar
$^1/_2$ cup butter or
    margarine, softened
2 eggs
juice of 1 orange
1 tbsp. zest or grated
    orange peel

2 cups flour
1 tsp. baking soda
$^1/_2$ tsp. salt
1 cup buttermilk
$^3/_4$ cup chopped dried cherries
2 tbsp. sugar
$^1/_4$ cup chopped walnuts

Cream sugar and butter until smooth with electric mixer. Add eggs and zest, beating until fluffy. Combine flour, soda, and salt; add to creamed mixture, alternating with buttermilk. Add cherries, stirring until well mixed. Spoon batter into greased muffin tins, filling 2/3 full. Bake in 400 degree oven for 20 minutes. Remove pan from oven and brush muffins with orange juice and sprinkle with sugar while still warm. Allow to stand in pan 5 minutes before removing. Yield: 12 muffins.

FOR MINIATURE MUFFINS: Spoon batter into greased 1 3/4-inch muffin tins. Bake in 400 degree oven for 10 to 12 minutes. Yield: 36-40 muffins.

Cranberry Muffins

$^1/_2$ cup butter or
    margarine, softened
$^3/_4$ cup sugar
2 eggs
2 cups flour
$2^3/_4$ tsp. baking powder

1 tsp. cinnamon
$^1/_2$ tsp. salt
1 can (16 oz.) whole
    cranberry sauce
1 cup chopped walnuts

Heat oven to 350 degrees. Grease muffin tins or line with baking papers. In medium bowl, beat butter until creamy. Beat in sugar until light and fluffy. Add eggs one at a time. In a small bowl mix flour, baking powder, cinnamon, and salt. Mix into margarine mixture. Fold in cranberry sauce and walnuts. Spoon into muffin tins. Bake until toothpick inserted comes out clean, approximately 25 minutes.

Cranberry Banana Nut Muffins

2 eggs, lightly beaten
3 tbsp. butter, softened
3 tbsp. honey
3 tbsp. molasses
3 tbsp. orange or apple
   juice concentrate
1 tsp. vanilla extract
$^3/_4$ cup mashed banana
$1^1/_4$ cup fresh or dried
   chopped cranberries

$^1/_2$ cup chopped nuts
1 cup sifted whole wheat flour
2 tbsp. wheat bran
2 tbsp. wheat germ
$^1/_4$ cup oat bran
1 tbsp. grated orange rind
$^1/_2$ tsp. baking powder
$^1/_2$ tsp. baking soda

Preheat oven to 375 degrees. In a large mixing bowl or food processor, blend together the eggs, butter, honey, molasses, juice concentrate, vanilla extract, and mashed banana. Add the chopped cranberries and nuts. In another bowl, combine the wheat flour, wheat bran, wheat germ, oat bran, orange rind, baking powder, and baking soda. Grease twelve muffin tins. Spoon the batter into the tins and bake for 20 to 25 minutes or until golden and crusty.

Famous Cranberry Orange Muffins

2 cups flour
1 cup sugar
3 tsp. baking powder
1 tsp. salt
$1/2$ tsp. baking soda
$1/4$ cup applesauce

1 beaten egg
1 tbsp. grated orange peel
$3/4$ cup orange juice
$1^1/2$ cups golden raisins
$1^1/2$ cups cranberries, chopped

Mix all ingredients together, until slightly moistened. Spoon batter into prepared muffin tins. Bake at 350 degrees for about 25 to 30 minutes.

Date Nut Muffins

$1^1/4$ cup whole wheat flour
$1/2$ tsp. salt
2 tsp. baking powder
$1/2$ cup chopped dates
$1/2$ cup chopped nuts
$1/2$ cup wheat germ

3 tbsp. light molasses
2 tbsp. oil
1 cup apple juice
1 tsp. grated lemon rind
$1/2$ tsp. allspice

Preheat oven to 375 degrees. Prepare muffin tins. Sift the flour, baking powder, salt, and baking soda. Stir in the dates, nuts, and wheat germ. Beat the remaining ingredients together until smooth; then combine both mixtures, stirring until smooth. Spoon into muffin tins. Bake 15 to 20 minutes. Yield: 12 muffins

Date Raisin Muffins

1 cup sliced almonds
3 to 4 extra ripe
   bananas, peeled
1 cup canned pumpkin
3 eggs
1^1/$_2$ tsp. allspice cups sugar
1 cup vegetable oil

5 cups flour
1 tbsp. baking soda
2 tsp. cinnamon
1 tsp. ground cloves
1 cup chopped dates
1 cup raisins

Puree bananas (2 cups). Combine bananas, pumpkin, eggs, and sugar in a bowl. Beat in oil. Combine dry ingredients in separate bowl; beat into banana mixture. Fold in dates and raisins. Spoon 1/4 cup batter into paper-lined muffin tins. Bake in 350 degree oven for 25 minutes. Cool. Yield: 24-30 muffins

Huckleberry Muffins

2 cups flour
4 tsp. baking powder
^{1}/$_4$ tsp. salt
^{1}/$_3$ cup sugar

2 tbsp. butter, melted
1 egg
1 cup milk
1 cup huckleberries

Sift flour; measure and reserve 3 tablespoons to dust berries. To remaining flour add baking powder, salt, and sugar. Sift again. Add beaten egg and melted butter to milk; combine with dry ingredients. Fold in berries. Spoon into greased muffin tins. Bake at 400 degrees for 25 minutes. Yield: 12-15 muffins

Lemon Blueberry Muffins

2 cups flour	1 cup light cream
1 cup sugar	$^1/_2$ cup vegetable oil
1 tbsp. baking powder	1 tsp. lemon extract
$^1/_4$ tsp. salt	$1^1/_2$ cups fresh or
2 eggs, lightly beaten	frozen blueberries

Combine flour, sugar, baking powder, and salt. Combine eggs, cream, oil, and lemon extract. Stir egg mixture into flour mixture just until moistened. Fold in blueberries. Fill muffin tins 2/3 full. Bake at 400 degrees for approx. 20 minutes. Yield: 18 muffins

Lemon Raspberry Muffins

2 cups flour	1 cup light cream
1 cup sugar	$^1/_2$ cup vegetable oil
1 tbsp. baking powder	$^3/_4$ tsp. lemon extract
$^1/_4$ tsp. salt	$1^1/_2$ cups fresh or
2 eggs, lightly beaten	frozen raspberries

In a large bowl combine flour, sugar, baking powder, and salt. Combine the eggs, cream, oil, and lemon extract; stir into dry ingredients just until moistened. Fold in raspberries. Spoon into greased or paper-lined muffin tins. Bake at 400 degrees for 18 to 20 minutes or until golden brown. Yield: 18 muffins

Papaya Cashew Muffins

$1/2$ cup dried papaya, diced
$3/4$ cup apple or
    apple-apricot juice
2 eggs
2 tbsp. olive oil
2 tbsp. molasses
1 tbsp. honey
2 tbsp. wheat bran
1 cup sifted whole wheat flour

2 tbsp. wheat germ
$1/2$ tsp. baking soda
1 tsp. baking powder
1 tsp. cinnamon
$1/8$ tsp. nutmeg
pinch of ginger
$2/3$ cup sliced, salted
    & roasted cashews

Combine wet and dry ingredients. Add cashews. Fill prepared muffin tins 2/3 full. Bake at 400 degrees for 20 minutes.

To test a fruit for ripeness, stick a toothpick in the fruit at the stem end. If it goes in and out clean and with ease, the fruit is ripe and ready to be eaten.

Peanut Butter Banana Muffins

$^2/_3$ cup peanut butter
$^1/_2$ cup mashed banana
$^3/_4$ cup yogurt or buttermilk
3 tbsp. honey
1 tsp. vanilla extract
2 eggs
1$^1/_2$ cups sifted
   whole wheat flour

1 tsp. cinnamon
1 tsp. baking powder
1 tsp. baking soda
4 tbsp. unsweetened blackberry
   or strawberry conserve
$^1/_4$ cup chopped peanuts

Preheat oven to 400 degrees. In a bowl mix together the peanut butter, bananas, yogurt or buttermilk, honey, vanilla, and the eggs. In another bowl, combine the flours, cinnamon, baking powder, and baking soda. Mix to combine the wet and dry ingredients. Half fill the greased muffin tins, top with a teaspoon of conserve, then top with the remaining batter. Sprinkle with peanuts. Bake in the upper half of the oven for 20 to 25 minutes. Yield: 12 muffins.

Whole wheat flour will last up to 4 months after purchase if kept refrigerated.

Pear Walnut Muffins

2 cups flour
$1/2$ cup firmly packed
   brown sugar
1 tsp. baking soda
$1/4$ tsp salt
1 tsp. cinnamon
$1/4$ tsp. ground nutmeg

$1/8$ tsp. ground cloves
1 cup plain lowfat yogurt
$1/2$ cup vegetable oil
3 tbsp. molasses
1 egg, lightly beaten
$1\,1/2$ cups diced pears
$1/2$ cup chopped walnuts

Preheat oven to 400 degrees. In a large bowl, stir together flour, brown sugar, baking soda, salt, cinnamon, nutmeg, and cloves. In another bowl, stir together yogurt, oil, molasses, and egg until blended. Make a well in center of dry ingredients; add yogurt mixture and stir just to combine. Stir in pears and walnuts. Spoon batter into greased muffin tins. Bake 20 to 25 minutes or until toothpick inserted in center of one muffin comes out clean. Cool 5 minutes before removing muffins from tins; finish cooling on rack. Serve warm or cool completely and store in airtight container at room temperature. (These muffins freeze well.) Yield: 12 muffins

Blackstrap Molasses is higher in nutrients than other types of molasses. It's high in Iron, Calcium and Potassium.

Pineapple Almond Muffins

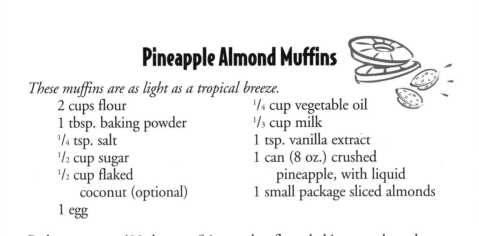

These muffins are as light as a tropical breeze.

2 cups flour
1 tbsp. baking powder
$^{1}/_{4}$ tsp. salt
$^{1}/_{2}$ cup sugar
$^{1}/_{2}$ cup flaked
   coconut (optional)
1 egg

$^{1}/_{4}$ cup vegetable oil
$^{1}/_{3}$ cup milk
1 tsp. vanilla extract
1 can (8 oz.) crushed
   pineapple, with liquid
1 small package sliced almonds

Preheat oven to 400 degrees. Stir together flour, baking powder, salt, sugar, and coconut. Combine egg, oil, milk, vanilla, and pineapple; mix well. Add this mixture to dry ingredients. Stir just until moistened. Fill greased or paper-lined muffin tins 2/3 full. If desired, sprinkle sliced almonds over batter and press them in lightly. Bake for 20 minutes or until golden brown. Yield: 14 muffins

One ounce of almonds have as much calcium as 1/4 cup of milk.

Rhubarb Muffins

In large bowl combine and mix well:

2 eggs
1 cup sugar
$^1/_2$ cup vegetable oil
$^1/_2$ cup plain yogurt

1 tsp. vanilla extract
$1^2/_3$ cups fresh
    rhubarb, chopped

In smaller bowl combine and mix well:

2 cups flour
2 tsp. baking powder
$^1/_2$ tsp. baking soda

$^1/_4$ tsp. salt
$^1/_2$ tsp. cinnamon

Combine wet and dry mixtures; fold together gently until just mixed. Spoon into prepared muffin tins. Bake at 375 degrees for 25 minutes.

To remove muffins more easily, try placing the tin directly from the oven onto a wet towel for 20-30 seconds.

Rhubarb Orange Muffins

In large bowl combine and mix well:

2 eggs	1/2 cup plain yogurt
1 cup sugar	1 tsp. vanilla extract
1/4 cup vegetable oil	1 2/3 cups fresh rhubarb, chopped

In smaller bowl combine and mix well:

2 cups flour	1/4 tsp. salt
2 tsp. baking powder	1/2 tsp. mace
1/2 tsp. baking soda	1 tsp. grated orange peel

Combine wet and dry mixtures; fold together gently until just mixed.
Spoon into prepared muffin tins. Bake at 375 degrees for 20 to 25 minutes.

 # Strawberry Rhubarb Muffins

In large bowl combine and mix well:

2 eggs	1 cup fresh rhubarb,
1 cup sugar	chopped, lightly packed
1/4 cup vegetable oil	3/4 cup fresh
1/2 cup plain yogurt	strawberries, chopped
1 tsp. vanilla extract	

In smaller bowl combine and mix well:

2 cups flour	1/2 tsp. baking soda
2 tsp. baking powder	1/4 tsp. salt

Combine wet and dry mixtures; fold together gently until just mixed.
Spoon into prepared muffin tins. Bake at 375 degrees for 25 minutes.

Carrot Muffins

1¹/₂ cups flour
³/₄ cup sugar
2¹/₂ tsp. baking powder
1¹/₂ tsp. cinnamon
¹/₂ tsp. nutmeg

2 eggs, beaten
¹/₂ cup vegetable oil
¹/₈ cup milk
1¹/₂ cups carrots, coarsely grated

In a large bowl combine flour, sugar, baking powder, cinnamon, and nutmeg. In a medium bowl combine eggs, oil, milk, and carrots. Pour wet ingredients into dry mixture; stir just until moist. Fill greased muffin tins half full. Bake at 400 degrees for 18 to 20 minutes or until top of muffins spring up. Yield: 12 muffins

George's "Secret" Carrot Muffins

A secret ingredient makes these muffins extra moist and delicious!

4 eggs
1¹/₂ cups sugar
¹/₂ cup brown sugar
3 jars (7¹/₂ oz.) junior
    carrot baby food
¹/₄ cup vegetable oil
    or applesauce

2 cups flour
2 tsp. baking soda
1 tsp. salt
3 tsp. cinnamon
1 cup raisins (optional)

Mix dry ingredients. Mix wet ingredients in separate bowl; add to dry mixture. Fill muffin tins 3/4 full. Bake at 350 degrees for 30 minutes. Sprinkle cinnamon sugar on top while hot.

Carrot-Date-Nut Muffins

$1/4$ cup butter or margarine
$1/2$ cup honey
$1/2$ cup honey
2 eggs
$1 1/2$ cups flour

1 heaping tsp. baking powder
$1/2$ tsp. salt
1 cup grated carrots (2 medium)
1 cup pitted, chopped dates
$1/4$ cup finely chopped walnuts

Melt butter and honey. Stir in eggs and milk; beat. Combine dry ingredients and stir thoroughly. Stir in liquid mixture; fold in carrots, dates, and nuts. Bake at 375 degrees for 15 to 20 minutes. (Delicious when heated and served with butter, cream cheese or marmalade.

Carrot Pineapple Muffins

1 cup sugar
$2/3$ cup applesauce
2 eggs, beaten
$1 1/2$ cups flour
2 tsp. baking powder
1 tsp. baking soda
$1/8$ tsp. nutmeg

$1/2$ tsp. cinnamon
$1/4$ tsp. salt
1 tsp. vanilla extract
1 cup finely grated carrot
1 cup crushed pineapple,
    drained

In beater bowl, combine sugar, oil, and beaten eggs. In another bowl, combine flour, baking powder, baking soda, nutmeg, cinnamon, and salt; mix well. Add dry ingredients to the sugar and oil mixture; stir to moisten. Add grated carrots, pineapple, and vanilla. Fill greased muffin tins to the top. Bake at 375 degrees for 20 minutes. Option: chopped nuts may be added, if desired.

made for Rachel's preschool snack 1/3/00

Carrot Orange Pecan Muffins

2 eggs
$1/2$ cup frozen orange
   juice concentrate
3 tbsp. butter, softened
$1/4$ cup plain yogurt
$1^1/2$ cups grated carrots
1 cup chopped pecans
$1^1/4$ cups sifted
   whole wheat flour

$1/4$ cup wheat germ
2 tbsp. lecithin granules
2 tbsp. oat bran
3 tsp. cinnamon
1 tbsp. grated orange rind
$1/2$ tsp. ground ginger
1 tsp. baking soda
1 tsp. baking powder

In a large bowl or food processor blend together the eggs, orange juice concentrate, butter, yogurt, and grated carrots. Mix in the pecans. In another bowl stir together the flour, wheat germ, lecithin, oat bran, cinnamon, orange rind, ginger, baking soda, and baking powder. Preheat oven to 375 degrees. Spoon into greased muffin tins. Bake 20-25 minutes. Yield: 12 muffins

Lecithin granules are available at most natural food stores. Lecithin is said to lower cholesterol and improve memory.

Carrot Prune Muffins

$1/4$ cup honey
3 tbsp. vegetable oil
$1/2$ tsp. cinnamon
1 cup water
2 tbsp. lemon juice
$1^1/2$ cups whole wheat flour
$3/4$ cup whole wheat
    bread flour

$2^1/2$ tsp. baking powder
$1/2$ tsp. salt
$1/2$ tsp. baking soda
$1/2$ cup wheat germ
1 cup grated carrots
$3/4$ cup pitted prunes
$1/2$ cup chopped nuts

Preheat oven to 350 degrees. Prepare muffin tins. Beat honey, oil, and cinnamon with a fork. Stir in the water and lemon juice. Sift dry ingredients together, adding the wheat germ at the end. Add the dry ingredients to the liquid ingredients; mixing just enough to combine. Fold in carrots, prunes, and nuts. Spoon into muffin tins. Bake 20 minutes.

APRICOT PRUNE MUFFINS: Soften 3/4 cup dried apricots in 2 cups very hot water. Drain, saving 1 1/4 cups of the liquid to use for the water measure in the muffins. Chop the apricots and substitute them for the carrots. Omit the lemon juice.

If you are chopping nuts in a blender, add a small amount of sugar and they won't clump together.

Carrot and Zucchini Muffins

$1^1/_2$ cups whole wheat flour
1 tsp. salt
$1^1/_2$ tsp. baking soda
1 tsp. cinnamon
$1^1/_2$ tsp. nutmeg
$1^1/_2$ cups natural bran
$^1/_2$ cup grated carrots
$^1/_2$ cup grated zucchini

2 eggs
$^1/_4$ cup vegetable oil
$1^1/_2$ cups skim milk or
    orange juice
2 tbsp. vinegar
$^1/_2$ cup honey
$^1/_4$ cup molasses
$^1/_2$ cup raisins

Blend the flour, salt, baking soda, cinnamon, nutmeg, and bran together. Add carrots and zucchini to dry ingredients. Stir together remaining ingredients; add to dry ingredients. Do not over mix, stir until blended. Bake at 375 degrees for 20 to 25 minutes.

Paul's Favorite Pumpkin Muffins

$1^1/_2$ cups flour
$^1/_2$ cup sugar
2 tsp. baking powder
$^3/_4$ tsp. salt
$^1/_2$ tsp. cinnamon
$^1/_2$ tsp. nutmeg

4 tbsp. butter, softened
$^1/_2$ cup raisins
$^1/_2$ cup pumpkin
$^1/_2$ cup milk
1 egg

In large bowl mix flour, sugar, baking powder, salt, cinnamon, and nutmeg. In smaller bowl blend softened butter, raisins, pumpkin, milk, and eggs; add to dry ingredients. Mix well. Bake at 450 degrees for 18 to 20 minutes.

Real Corn Cornbread Muffins

1 cup whole wheat flour
1 cup cornmeal
$^1/_4$ cup sugar
1 tbsp. baking powder

2 eggs
1 can corn (12 oz.), drained
$1^1/_4$ cups milk
$^1/_4$ cup vegetable oil

Preheat oven to 425 degrees. Line muffin tins. Mix dry ingredients in a large bowl. Beat eggs in a smaller bowl, add milk, oil, and corn. Add liquid ingredients to dry ingredients. Mix well. Bake for 20 minutes.

HOT MUFFINS: Add 1 small can chopped jalapeño peppers.

CHEESY CORN MUFFINS: Add 1/2 cup shredded, extra sharp cheddar cheese.

VEGGY MUFFINS: Substitute 1 can of mixed vegetables for the canned corn.

Zucchini Cheese Muffins

2 tbsp. minced onion
2 tbsp. vegetable oil
1 egg, lightly beaten
$^1/_2$ cup oat flakes
$^1/_2$ cup grated cheddar cheese

$1^1/_2$ cups grated zucchini
$^2/_3$ cup water
$1^1/_2$ cups rye flour
$^1/_2$ tsp. salt
$2^1/_2$ tsp. baking powder

Preheat oven to 375 degrees. Prepare 12 muffin tins. Saute the onions in oil. Mix the egg, oil, onion, and oats together. Stir in cheese, zucchini, and water. Sift together flour, salt, and baking powder. Add the dry ingredients to the zucchini mixture; stirring just enough to mix. Spoon into muffin tins. Bake for 20 minutes.

grain muffins

Apple Bran Muffins

2 cups bran flake cereal
1 cup milk
1$^1/_2$ cups flour
2 tbsp. sugar
2 tsp. baking powder
1 tsp. cinnamon
$^1/_4$ tsp. salt

2 eggs, lightly beaten
$^1/_2$ cup applesauce
3 tbsp. vegetable oil
1 tsp. vanilla extract
$^1/_2$ cup toasted chopped almonds
$^1/_2$ cup chopped dates
$^1/_2$ cup raisins

Preheat oven to 400 degrees. Line muffin tins with paper liners. In large bowl combine bran flakes and milk; let stand 5 minutes. In separate bowl combine flour, sugar, baking powder, cinnamon, and salt; set aside. Add eggs, applesauce, oil, and vanilla to bran flakes; beat well. Stir in dry ingredients, almonds, dates, and raisins; just until moistened. Fill muffin tins 3/4 full. Bake 25 to 30 minutes. Yield: 12 muffins at 180 calories each.

*Toasting intensifies the flavor
and adds crispness to nuts.*

Banana Bran Muffins

1 egg
$^3/_4$ cup brown sugar
4 mashed bananas
$^1/_2$ cup raisins
$^1/_3$ cup vegetable oil
1 tsp. vanilla extract
$^3/_4$ cup all-purpose flour

$^3/_4$ cup whole wheat flour
$^1/_2$ cup oat bran
2 tsp. baking powder
$^1/_2$ tsp. baking soda
1 tsp. cinnamon
$^1/_4$ tsp. salt

Mix all ingredients together. Spoon batter into prepared muffin tins. Bake at 375 degrees for 20 to 25 minutes.

Banana Oatmeal Muffins

$^3/_4$ cup sugar
1 cup mashed ripe banana
2 cups whole wheat flour
2 tbsp. baking powder
$^1/_2$ tsp. salt
$^1/_2$ tsp. baking soda

$^1/_2$ tsp. cinnamon
$^1/_4$ tsp. nutmeg
1 cup quick cooking oats
2 eggs, well beaten
1 cup milk
$^1/_4$ cup vegetable oil

In a large bowl stir together sugar, flour, baking powder, salt, baking soda, cinnamon, and nutmeg. Stir in oats and banana. In separate bowl stir together eggs, milk, and oil; add to flour mixture. Stir to moisten. Bake at 350 degrees for 30 to 35 minutes.

Blueberry Bran Muffins

This recipe makes 3 dozen muffins, but leftovers freeze well. For best results, make batter one day ahead.

6 eggs
1¹/₂ cups firmly packed
   brown sugar
¹/₄ cup light molasses
¹/₄ cup honey
4 cups buttermilk
1¹/₂ cups vegetable oil
1 tsp. vanilla extract
2¹/₂ cups bran flakes
2 cups wheat germ

1³/₄ cups finely chopped
   pecans or walnuts
2 cups fresh or
   frozen blueberries
4¹/₄ cups flour
4 tsp. baking powder
4 tsp. baking soda
1 tbsp. cinnamon
¹/₄ tsp. salt

Using mixer, beat eggs with sugar, molasses, and honey in a large bowl until blended. Mix in buttermilk, oil, and vanilla; then add bran, wheat germ, and 1 1/4 cups of the nuts. Let batter stand 10 minutes at room temperature.

Stir berries into batter. Mix flour, baking powder, baking soda, cinnamon, and salt in medium bowl. Add to batter and mix until just combined. Cover and refrigerate overnight.

Preheat oven to 400 degrees. Line muffin tins with paper liners. Spoon 1/4 cup batter into each tin. Sprinkle tops with remaining nuts. Bake for 25 minutes.

Bran Muffins

1 cup whole wheat flour	2 tbsp. brown sugar
1 tsp. baking soda	2 tbsp. molasses
$1/2$ tsp. salt	1 egg
$1^1/2$ cup bran	$1^1/2$ cups buttermilk
3 tbsp. vegetable oil	

Preheat oven to 375 degrees. Prepare muffin tins. In small bowl stir flour, soda, and salt together; stir in the bran. In large bowl beat oil, sugar, and molasses together; add eggs and buttermilk. Mix dry ingredients into liquids. Fill muffin tins 3/4 full. Bake 15 to 20 minutes.

OPTIONAL: Add one of the following ingredients before spooning batter into tins:

$1/2$ cup raisins
$1/2$ cup currants
$1/2$ cup dates
$1/2$ cup nuts
$1/2$ cup blueberries (fresh)
$1/2$ cup chopped dried apricots

Buttermilk contains only 1% milk fat.

Cornflake Muffins

Great "on-the-go" breakfast

3 cups cornflake crumbs
3 cups milk
$^2/_3$ cup sugar
$^3/_4$ cup butter (1$^1/_2$ sticks)
3 eggs
2 tsp. vanilla

3 cups flour
1 tsp. cinnamon
1$^1/_4$ tsp. salt
2 tsp. baking powder
Your favorite
    jam or jelly

Preheat oven 400°. In a large bowl soak cornflake crumbs in milk for about 10 minutes. In another bowl beat sugar and butter together until fluffy. Stir in eggs and vanilla. Add to cornflake mixture. In separate bowl mix flour, baking powder, cinnamon and salt. Blend into cornflake mixture. Bake 20-25 minutes. Serve warm with your favorite jam or jelly.

Millet Crunch Muffins

1 cup white flour
1 cup whole wheat flour
3 tsp. baking powder
$1/4$ tsp. salt
$1/2$ cup whole millet

1 cup milk
$1/4$ cup honey
$1/3$ cup butter, melted
2 eggs, slightly beaten

Preheat oven 400°. Mix dry ingredients in large bowl. In smaller bowl mix wet ingredients. Combine mixtures and stir just until moistened. Spoon into prepared muffin tins and bake 20-25 minutes.

Millet is found in most health food stores and is a great source of protein.

Honey Bran Muffins

1 cup natural bran
1 cup buttermilk
1/3 cup butter or margarine,
   softened
1/2 cup brown sugar
3 tsp. honey

1 egg
1 cup flour
2 tsp. baking powder
1/2 tsp. baking soda
1/2 tsp. salt

Soak bran in buttermilk while preparing the rest. Cream butter and brown sugar. Beat in the honey and egg. Add the bran and buttermilk. Stir together the flour, baking powder, baking soda, and salt. Add dry ingredients and stir until moistened. Bake 375 degrees for 15 to 20 minutes.

Peanut Butter Bran Muffins

1 1/4 cups flour
1/4 cup sugar
1 tbsp. baking powder
1 tsp. salt

1 1/2 cups bran cereal
1/2 cup peanut butter
1 egg
1/2 cup raisins

Topping:
   2 T. brown sugar

1/2 tsp. cinnamon

Mix flour, sugar. baking powder, and salt. In a medium bowl, mix cereal and milk; let stand until softened. Stir in peanut butter, eggs, and raisins. Stir in flour mixture. Sprinkle muffins with topping. Bake at 400 degrees for 25 to 30 minutes.

Pineapple Bran Whole Wheat Muffins

1 cup whole wheat flour
1 tsp. baking powder
$1/4$ tsp. salt
$1^1/2$ tbsp. brown sugar
1 egg

1 cup 100% all bran cereal
$1/3$ cup skim milk
$1/4$ cup vegetable oil
1 can (8 oz.) crushed
    pineapple, undrained

Mix the flour, baking powder, salt, and sugar. Beat the egg lightly. Add the cereal, milk, and oil to the egg. Stir to combine. Let stand for 2 minutes or until cereal is softened. Stir the pineapple, including the juice, into the mixture. Add the flour mixture stirring only until combined. Spoon batter into paper-lined muffin tins. Bake at 400 degrees for 25 minutes.

No Fat Bran Muffins

1 cup white flour
2 cups bran
$1/4$ cup cornmeal
1 tsp. salt
$1^1/4$ cups skim milk

$1/2$ cup molasses
1 tsp. baking soda, dissolved
    in a little water
1 cup raisins

Mix all ingredients together. Pour into paper-lined muffin tins. Bake at 325 degrees for 25 minutes.

Perpetual Microwave Bran Muffins

2 cups All-Bran Cereal
1 cup 100% Bran
1 cup boiling water
2 cups skim milk (soured
    with 1 tbsp. lemon juice)
$1^1/_2$ cups sugar
3 egg whites, beaten

$^1/_2$ cup applesauce
1 cup all-purpose flour
1 cup whole wheat flour
$^3/_4$ cup oatmeal
$2^1/_2$ tsp. baking soda
2 tsp. baking powder
$^1/_2$ tsp. salt

Pour hot water over cereals. Stir in ingredients one by one until blended. Store in refrigerator until ready to cook muffins. (Batter may be stored up to six weeks.) For an easy treat, muffins may be microwaved in a coffee cup. Simply fill cup 1/4 to 1/3 full and microwave on high for 1 to 1 1/2 minutes. Or, fill glass muffin cup 1/3 full and microwave on high for 2 to 3 minutes.

When washing muffin tins in which muffins have stuck or burned, try turning the pan upside down in steaming sudsy water and food will loosen in a very short time.

The Very Best Raisin Bran Muffins

Makes enough batter for 48 muffins. Batter will keep in the refrigerator for several weeks.

1 cup margarine
1 cup sugar
1 cup firmly packed
   brown sugar
4 eggs, beaten
4 cups buttermilk

5 cups whole wheat flour
1 box raisin bran cereal (15 oz.)
1 cup raisins
5 tsp. baking soda
2 tsp. salt

Preheat oven to 400 degrees. Line muffin tins with paper. Mix margarine and sugars in a large bowl. Stir in eggs. Gradually add buttermilk. Add remaining ingredients and mix. Fill tins 3/4 full. Bake for 20 minutes. Chill remaining batter in an air tight container.

Whole Wheat Carrot Muffins

$1^1/_4$ cups whole wheat flour
$^1/_4$ cup all-purpose flour
2 tsp. baking powder
$^1/_4$ tsp. salt
2 eggs

1 cup plain lowfat yogurt
2 tbsp. molasses
1 tbsp. vegetable oil
$^1/_2$ cup shredded carrots

In a large bowl, stir together flours, baking powder, and salt. In a small bowl beat the eggs with a fork; beat in the yogurt, molasses, and oil; stir in the carrots. Add the flour mixture; stir until moistened. Spoon batter into paper-lined muffin tins. Bake at 375 degrees for 15 to 20 minutes.

Corn Muffins

1¹/₂ cups flour
³/₄ cup yellow cornmeal
¹/₄ cup sugar
1 tbsp. baking powder
¹/₂ tsp. salt

2 eggs
1 cup milk
¹/₂ cup vegetable oil
1 tbsp. molasses

In large bowl combine flour, cornmeal, sugar, baking powder, and salt. In medium bowl whisk eggs, milk, molasses, and oil. Pour wet ingredients into dry mixture; stir just until moist. Spoon batter into greased muffin tins. Bake at 350 degrees for 20 minutes or until golden brown. Yield: 12 muffins

Honey Corn Muffins

1³/₄ cups flour
³/₄ cup cornmeal
1 tbsp. baking powder
1 tbsp. baking soda
1 tsp. salt

¹/₂ cup buttermilk
¹/₄ cup orange juice
¹/₄ cup vegetable oil
¹/₄ cup honey

Preheat oven to 350 degrees. In a large bowl combine flour, cornmeal, sugar, baking powder, soda, and salt. In a small bowl blend buttermilk, orange juice, oil, and honey; add to dry ingredients. Stir until moistened. Pour batter into paper-lined muffin tins. Bake for 15 minutes.

Peanutty Corn Muffins

$^3/_4$ cup whole wheat flour
1 tsp. baking powder
$^1/_2$ tsp. salt
$^3/_4$ cup cornmeal
$^1/_4$ cup roasted peanuts,
    finely chopped

1 tbsp. vegetable oil
$^1/_4$ cup crunchy peanut butter
2 tbsp. honey
$1^1/_2$ cups buttermilk
1 egg, lightly beaten

Preheat oven to 375 degrees. Prepare muffin tins. Sift flour, baking powder, soda, and salt; stir in the peanuts and cornmeal. In separate bowl beat together oil, peanut butter, and honey; add buttermilk and egg. Stir dry ingredients into wet ingredients; mixing until almost smooth. Spoon batter into muffin tins. If desired, sprinkle more peanuts on top of the muffins. Bake 12 to 15 minutes. Yield: 12 muffins

Corn Rye Muffins

$1^1/_2$ cups rye flour
1 cup cornmeal
$2^1/_2$ tsp. baking powder
$^1/_2$ tsp. baking soda
$^3/_4$ tbsp. caraway seed

3 tbsp. molasses
3 tbsp. vegetable oil
1 egg
$1^1/_4$ cups buttermilk

Preheat oven to 350 degrees. Prepare muffin tins. Sift the dry ingredients together; add caraway seed. In a separate bowl beat the oil, molasses, and egg together; stir in the buttermilk. Add the dry ingredients to the wet ingredients; stirring just to mix. Spoon batter into muffin tins. Bake for 15 minutes.

Oatmeal Cherry Muffins

Perfect for breakfast or lunchbox treats, these muffins are low in fat and calories.

1 cup old-fashioned or quick
  cooking oats, uncooked
1 cup flour
$^1/_2$ cup firmly packed
  brown sugar
$1^1/_2$ tsp. baking powder
$^1/_8$ tsp. ground nutmeg

$^3/_4$ cup buttermilk
1 egg, lightly beaten
$^1/_4$ cup applesauce
1 tsp. vanilla extract
1 cup chopped and pitted
  cherries, fresh or frozen

In a large mixing bowl, combine oats, flour, brown sugar, baking powder, and nutmeg. In a small bowl, combine buttermilk, egg, oil, and vanilla. Pour buttermilk mixture into oats mixture; stir just to moisten ingredients. Quickly stir in cherries (it is not necessary to thaw cherries before chopping and adding to batter). Prepare muffin tins. Fill tins 2/3 full. Bake in a preheated 400 degree oven 15 to 20 minutes. Yield: 12 muffins

NOTE: 1 cup canned tart cherries, drained and coarsely chopped, may be substituted for 1 cup frozen tart cherries.

Leave stems on cherries and they will stay fresh longer.

Oat Bran Cherry Muffins

2$^1/_4$ cups oat bran
$^1/_4$ cup brown sugar
1 tbsp. baking powder
2 egg whites, lightly beaten

1$^1/_4$ cups milk
2 tbsp. vegetable oil
1$^1/_4$ cups dried cherries
$^1/_4$ cup chopped pecans (optional)

Mix all ingredients together until dry ingredients are moistened. Spoon into muffin cups and bake at 425 degrees for 15 to 20 minutes. Yield: 18 muffins

Date Bran Muffins

1 egg
$^1/_4$ cup vegetable oil
1$^1/_3$ cups milk
1$^1/_3$ cups bran cereal
1 cup chopped dates

$^1/_2$ cup currants
1$^1/_2$ cups flour
1 tbsp. baking powder
$^1/_2$ cup sugar

Beat egg; add oil, milk, and cereal. Mix well. Set aside. Mix flour, baking powder, and sugar; add to cereal mixture. Stir in currants and dates. Bake at 400 degrees for 15 to 25 minutes.

Dates are one of the sweetest fruits. Most of the U.S. dates come from California or Arizona.

Cranberry Bran Muffins

$^3/_4$ cup whole bran cereal
$^3/_4$ cup milk
1 egg, lightly beaten
$^1/_4$ cup brown sugar
$^1/_4$ cup vegetable oil
$^1/_4$ cup wheat germ

$^1/_2$ tsp. baking powder
$^1/_2$ tsp. baking soda
$^1/_4$ tsp. salt
$^3/_4$ cup coarsely chopped
   cranberries

In a small bowl, combine bran cereal and milk. Let stand for 5 minutes. Stir in brown sugar, egg, and oil. In a medium bowl combine flour, wheat germ, baking powder, baking soda, and salt; add bran mixture. Stir until moistened. Add cranberries. Fill paper-lined muffin tins almost to the top. Sprinkle with crunchy topping. Bake at 400 degrees for 20 minutes.

CRUNCHY TOPPING: In a small bowl combine 2 tbsp. brown sugar, 2 tbsp. chopped pecans, 1 1/2 tbsp. wheat germ, 1 tbsp. flour and 1/4 tsp. cinnamon. Stir in 2 tbsp. melted butter.

To make sure your baking powder is fresh, try pouring very hot tap water over a teaspoonful. If it's fresh it will bubble very actively.

Bettey's "A Little Bit of Everything" Muffins

2 cups bran flake cereal
$^2/_3$ cup milk
$^1/_2$ cup mashed ripe banana,
 canned pumpkin,
 applesauce, finely diced
 peaches or smooth
 pineapple sauce
1 cup flour, white or
 whole wheat
$^1/_2$ cup oat bran
1 tbsp. baking powder

$^1/_2$ tsp. salt
$^1/_4$ cup vegetable oil
1 egg, lightly beaten
$^1/_2$ cup raisins
$^1/_2$ cup chopped nuts,
 walnuts, almonds or pecans
$^1/_4$ cup sunflower seeds
$^1/_4$ cup chopped dates
$^1/_4$ cup coconut
$^1/_4$ cup sugar (optional)

Topping
Mix together:
$^1/_2$ cup brown sugar
$^1/_4$ cup finely chopped nuts

$^1/_4$ cup coconut
$^1/_4$ cup sunflower seeds

Preheat oven to 350 degrees. Line muffin tins with paper. Mix cereal, milk, and fruit. Set aside. Mix flour, oat bran, baking powder, salt, and sugar (optional). Add cereal to flour mixture. Stir in oil and egg. Mix well. Add remaining ingredients. Fill muffin tins 3/4 full. Sprinkle topping on muffins. Bake until golden brown.

Graham Muffins

2 tsp. lemon juice
1 cup milk
$^1/_2$ tsp. baking soda
1 egg
3 tbsp. molasses

2 tbsp. honey
2 tbsp. butter, melted
2 cups plus 2 tbsp. graham flour
$^1/_2$ tsp. salt

Preheat oven to 400 degrees. Prepare muffin tins. Mix the lemon juice with the milk and set in a warm oven for a few minutes to sour. Stir the baking soda into the sour milk. Beat the egg lightly in a large bowl; add the molasses, honey, melted butter, and the sour milk. Blend in the flour and salt, mixing just enough to thoroughly moisten the dry ingredients. Spoon batter into the muffin tins, and bake for 12 to 15 minutes. Yield: 24 muffins

Graham Raisin Muffins

3 tbsp. sugar
3 tbsp. shortening
1 egg, lightly beaten
1 cup sour milk
1 cup all-purpose flour

$^3/_4$ cup graham flour
2 tsp. baking powder
$^1/_2$ tsp. baking soda
$^1/_4$ tsp. salt
$^3/_4$ cup raisins

Sift flours together; add baking powder, baking soda, and salt. Sift again. Cream shortening and sugar together. Add beaten egg. Add flour mixture alternately with milk. Add stewed raisins. Pour into greased muffin tins and bake at 400 degrees for 25 minutes. Yield: 12-15 muffins

Whole Wheat Ginger Orange Muffins

$^3/_4$ cup all-purpose flour
$^3/_4$ cup whole wheat flour
2/3 cup sugar
2 tsp. ginger
2 tsp. baking powder
$^1/_2$ tsp. baking soda
$^1/_4$ tsp. salt

$^1/_2$ cup raisins
1 tbsp. grated orange peel
7 tbsp. melted butter
$^1/_3$ cup sour cream
$^1/_3$ cup orange juice
2 eggs

In large bowl mix first seven ingredients. In small bowl mix wet ingredients; add wet ingredients to dry ingredients. Bake at 400 degrees for 20 to 25 minutes.

Health Muffins

2 cups raisins
2 cups water
2 cups graham flour
2 cups oatmeal
2 cups Bran Buds cereal

$1^1/_2$ cups sugar
1 tsp. salt
2 tsp. soda
2 cups milk (soured with
     1 tbsp. lemon juice)

Boil raisins in water for 5 minutes. Cool and add to remaining ingredients. Mix together. Bake at 350 degrees for about 30 minutes.

Granola Muffins

2 cups granola
1 cup flour
$^1/_3$ cup firmly packed
    brown sugar
2 tsp. baking powder
$^1/_2$ tsp. cinnamon
$^1/_4$ tsp. nutmeg
$^1/_2$ tsp. salt

$^1/_2$ cup milk
$^1/_3$ cup butter or margarine,
    melted and cooled
1 egg, lightly beaten
1 tsp. vanilla extract
$^1/_2$ cup raisins
$^1/_3$ cup slivered almonds
$^1/_3$ cup flaked coconut

Preheat oven to 400 degrees. Grease muffin tins. In a large bowl stir together granola, flour, brown sugar, baking powder, cinnamon, and salt. In another bowl stir together milk, butter, egg, and vanilla until blended. Make a well in center of dry ingredients; add milk mixture and stir just to combine. Stir in raisins, almonds, and coconut. Spoon batter into prepared muffin tins; bake 20 to 25 minutes or until cake tester inserted in center of one muffin comes out clean. Remove muffin tins from oven. Cool 5 minutes before removing muffins from tins; finish cooling on rack. These muffins freeze well. Yield: 12 muffins

Cinnamon is one of the oldest known spices. It's mentioned in the Bible several times.

Mover and Shaker Muffins

1 cup whole wheat flour
1 cup bran
2 tsp. baking powder
$^1/_2$ cup chopped pecans
1 egg

$1^1/_2$ cups buttermilk
$^1/_4$ cup molasses
2 tbsp. honey
2 tbsp. vegetable oil
$^1/_2$ cup chopped prunes

Preheat oven to 400 degrees. Line muffin tins. Thoroughly mix dry ingredients in large bowl; stir in prunes and pecans. In a separate bowl, beat egg and stir in buttermilk, molasses, honey, and vegetable oil. Add liquid ingredients to dry ingredients; stir until moistened. Bake 15 to 20 minutes.

Oat Bran Muffins

$2^1/_2$ cups oat bran (uncooked)
$^1/_4$ cup raisins or 1/4 cup
   chopped nuts (optional)
1 tsp. baking powder

$^3/_4$ cup milk
$^1/_3$ cup honey or maple syrup
2 tbsp. vegetable oil

Heat oven to 425 degrees. Coat muffin tins with vegetable oil and line with paper baking cups. In large bowl combine dry ingredients; mix well. In separate bowl blend liquids together, stirring slowly. Add to dry ingredients and stir until dry ingredients are moistened. Pour batter into prepared muffin tins until almost full. Bake approximately 15 minutes or until golden brown. Serve hot. Yield: 12 muffins

Oat Bran Applesauce Muffins

2¼ cups oat bran
½ cup chopped pecans
1 tsp. cinnamon
1 tsp. baking powder
½ tsp. baking soda
¼ tsp. salt

1 egg
1 cup apple sauce
½ cup packed brown sugar
½ cup plain yogurt
2 tbsp. vegetable oil

In large bowl combine oat bran, pecans, cinnamon, baking powder, baking soda, and salt. In a separate bowl whisk egg, applesauce, sugar, yogurt, and oil. Pour wet ingredients into dry mixture; stir just until moistened. Grease muffin tin and fill each cup 1/2 to 2/3 full. Bake at 350 degrees for 30 minutes or until golden brown. Yield: 8-12 muffins

The Best Oat Bran Muffins

1¾ cups oat bran
¼ cup flour
1 tsp. cinnamon
½ tsp. salt
½ tsp. baking soda
¼ tsp. baking powder
½ tsp. allspice

1 cup skim milk
1 container (6 oz.) frozen
    apple juice concentrate,
    thawed
½ cup raisins
2 large egg whites

Preheat oven to 350 degrees. Mix dry ingredients in bowl; stir in milk, juice, and raisins. Let stand 10 minutes. In separate bowl beat egg whites until soft peaks form; gently fold into batter. Pour batter into muffin cups lined with foil papers. Bake for 25 minutes. Yield: 18 muffins

Fruity Oat Bran Muffins

$2^1/_4$ cups oat bran
$^1/_2$ cup mixed diced dried fruits
1 tsp. cinnamon
1 tsp. baking powder
$^1/_2$ tsp. baking soda
$^1/_4$ tsp. salt

whites from 2 large eggs
1 cup unsweetened apple sauce
$^1/_2$ cup packed brown sugar
$^1/_2$ cup buttermilk or plain
    lowfat yogurt
2 tbsp. vegetable oil

Heat oven to 350 degrees. In medium bowl mix oat bran, fruit, cinnamon, baking powder, baking soda, and salt. In a large bowl mix remaining ingredients. Add oat bran mixture; stir well. Spoon 1/3 cup batter into each paper-lined muffin cup. Bake 30 to 35 minutes. Yield: 12 muffins

Grandma's Oat Bran Muffins

$2^1/_4$ cups oat bran
1 tbsp. baking powder
$^1/_4$ cup brown sugar
1 small can crushed
    pineapple (8 oz.)

2 egg whites
2 tbsp. canola oil
$^1/_2$ cup skim milk

Mix ingredients together; just until moistened. Bake at 350 degrees until firm and golden brown on top, approximately 20 minutes.

Oatmeal Muffins

1¹/₂ cup flour
2 tbsp. sugar
4 tsp. baking powder
¹/₂ tsp. salt
¹/₂ cup milk

1 egg, well beaten
2 tbsp. butter, melted
1 cup cooked oatmeal
1 cup raisins

Preheat oven to 400 degrees. Prepare muffin cups. In large bowl combine dry ingredients. In a separate bowl combine the milk, egg, and butter into the oatmeal; stir until well blended. Combine the two mixtures. Fill muffin cups 2/3 full. Bake for 20 minutes.

Oatmeal Apricot Muffins

1¹/₄ cups rolled oats
    (regular or instant)
1 cup flour
¹/₃ cup sugar
1 tbsp. baking powder
¹/₄ tsp. salt
²/₃ cup milk

1 jar (4.5 oz) apricot
    puree (baby food)
1 egg
¹/₄ cup vegetable oil
1 tsp. vanilla extract
²/₃ cup dried apricots, chopped

Combine first five ingredients in large bowl and mix well. Mix milk, apricot puree, egg, oil, and vanilla in another bowl. Add wet ingredients to dry; stir just until moistened. Fold in apricots. Fill greased muffin tins 2/3 full. Bake at 350 degrees for 20 minutes.

Oatmeal Carrot Muffins

1$\frac{1}{2}$ cups whole wheat flour
$\frac{1}{2}$ cup oatmeal
$\frac{1}{2}$ cup brown sugar
1 tbsp. baking powder
1 cup grated carrots

$\frac{1}{2}$ cup chopped walnuts
2 eggs
$\frac{1}{2}$ cup margarine, melted
$\frac{1}{2}$ cup milk

In large bowl combine dry ingredients; stir in carrots and walnuts. In a separate bowl beat eggs and mix in margarine and milk. Add to dry ingredients; stir until moistened. Bake at 400 degrees for 15 to 20 minutes.

Oatmeal Peach Muffins

$\frac{3}{4}$ cup sugar
1 can peaches (16 oz.)
2 cups whole wheat flour
2 tbsp. baking powder
1 tsp. salt
$\frac{1}{2}$ tsp. baking soda

$\frac{1}{2}$ tsp. cinnamon
$\frac{1}{4}$ tsp. nutmeg
1 cup quick oats
2 eggs, well beaten
1 cup milk
$\frac{1}{4}$ cup vegetable oil

Drain peaches and cut into small pieces. In large bowl stir together, sugar, flour, baking powder, salt, baking soda, cinnamon, and nutmeg. Stir in oats and peaches to coat. In separate bowl stir together eggs, milk, and oil; add to flour mixture. Stir to moisten. Bake at 350 degrees for 35 minutes.

Oatmeal Pineapple Muffins

³/₄ cup sugar
1 can crushed pineapple (8 oz.)
2 cups whole wheat flour
2 tbsp. baking powder
¹/₂ tsp. salt
¹/₂ tsp. baking soda

¹/₂ tsp. cinnamon
¹/₄ tsp. nutmeg
1 cup quick cooking oats
2 eggs, well beaten
1 cup milk
¹/₄ cup vegetable oil

Drain pineapple and cut into small pieces. In large bowl combine sugar, flour, baking powder, salt, baking soda, cinnamon, and nutmeg; stir well. Stir in oats and pineapple to coat. In separate bowl stir together eggs, milk, and oil; add to flour mixture. Stir to moisten. Bake at 350 degrees for 35 minutes.

Nutmeg and Mace are sister spices. They come from the same peach-like fruit. In commercial use, the seed of the fruit is Nutmeg and the lacy membrane surrounding the seed is Mace.

Oatmeal Prune Muffins

1 cup water
1$^1/_2$ cups chopped,
   pitted, dried prunes
$^2/_3$ cup uncooked old-
   fashioned rolled oats
$^1/_2$ cup margarine,
   melted and cooled
1$^1/_2$ cups flour

$^1/_2$ cup firmly packed brown sugar
$^1/_2$ cup sugar
1 tsp. baking soda
$^1/_4$ tsp. salt
1 tsp. cinnamon
$^1/_8$ tsp. ground nutmeg
2 eggs, lightly beaten
1$^1/_2$ tsp. vanilla extract

Preheat oven to 400 degrees. In a small saucepan, bring water to boil; remove from heat. Stir in prunes and oats; let stand 20 minutes. Stir in margarine; let stand 10 minutes or until cooled. In a large bowl stir together flour, brown sugar, baking soda, salt, cinnamon, and nutmeg. Stir eggs and vanilla into prune mixture in saucepan. Make a well in center of dry ingredients; add prune mixture and stir just to combine. Bake 20 to 25 minutes or until a cake tester inserted in center of one muffin comes out clean. Cool 5 minutes before removing muffins from tins. Yield: 12 muffins

According to the Food Guide Pyramid you should eat 6-11 servings from the bread, cereal, rice and pasta group – that includes muffins!

Oatmeal Raisin Muffins

1¹/₂ cups whole wheat flour
1 cup uncooked oatmeal
1 tbsp. baking powder
3 tbsp. sugar
¹/₂ cup raisins

¹/₂ cup walnuts, chopped
1 egg or 2 egg whites
1 cup non-fat milk
¹/₄ cup vegetable oil

Preheat oven to 400 degrees. In large bowl combine flour, oatmeal, baking powder, sugar, raisins, and nuts. In a separate bowl beat egg; stir in milk and oil. Add liquid mixture to flour mixture; stir just until blended. Pour batter into paper-lined muffin tins. Bake 15 to 20 minutes. Yield: 12 muffins

Oat-Nut Muffins

2 tsp. lemon juice
1¹/₂ cups milk
1 tsp. baking soda
2 cups rolled oats
2 eggS

6 tbsp. molasses
1¹/₂ cups flour
¹/₈ tsp. salt
¹/₂ cup chopped
    walnuts or pecans

Preheat oven to 400 degrees. Prepare muffin tins. Add the lemon juice to the milk and set in a warm oven to sour. Stir the baking soda into the sour milk. Place the rolled oats in a bowl, add the milk, and let stand 2 to 3 hours. Mix the eggs, molasses, flour, and salt into oats and milk. Blend just long enough to moisten the dry ingredients. Spoon the batter into tins. Bake 20 to 25 minutes. Yield: 16 muffins

Grandpa Taylor's Orange Corn Muffins

1 cup yellow cornmeal
1 cup flour
$^1/_3$ cup sugar
4 tsp. baking powder

$^1/_4$ tsp. salt
1 cup milk
$^1/_4$ cup vegetable oil
1 tbsp. grated orange peel

In a mixing bowl combine cornmeal, flour, sugar, baking powder, and salt. In another bowl combine egg, milk, oil, and orange peel. Add to cornmeal mixture; stirring just until ingredients are mixed. Fill greased muffin tins 2/3 full. Bake at 425 degrees for 15 minutes.

Tom's Pioneer Muffins

3 eggs
$^1/_4$ cup brown sugar
$^2/_3$ cup vegetable oil
$^1/_4$ cup molasses
2 cups bran
1 cup grated carrot
1 cup applesauce
$1^1/_2$ cups apple juice

$1^1/_2$ cups whole wheat flour
$^1/_2$ cup wheat germ
1 tsp. baking soda
2 tsp. baking powder
1 tsp. salt
1 tbsp. powdered milk
1 tbsp. cinnamon

In a large bowl beat eggs; add sugar, oil, molasses, bran, carrot, applesauce, and apple juice. Stir well. In medium bowl combine whole wheat flour, wheat germ, baking powder, baking soda, salt, milk, and cinnamon; mix well. Add dry ingredients to egg mixture; stir until moistened. Bake at 350 degrees for 20 to 25 minutes.

Honey Spice Rye Muffins

$^1/_3$ cup honey
$1^1/_3$ cups honey
3 tbsp. vegetable oil
2 tbsp. grated orange peel
$^3/_4$ tsp. salt
1 tsp. cinnamon
$^1/_2$ tsp. ground cloves
$^1/_2$ tsp. anise seed
$^1/_4$ tsp. ground ginger

$^1/_4$ tsp. ground allspice
2 tbsp. lemon juice
1 cup whole wheat flour
$1^1/_2$ cups rye flour
$2^1/_2$ tsp. baking powder
$^1/_2$ tsp. baking soda
$^1/_2$ cup chopped, toasted almonds
$^1/_2$ cup chopped dates

Preheat oven to 375 degrees. Combine the wet ingredients and the spices, beating them smooth with a fork. Sift the flours, baking powder, and soda. Add them gradually to the liquids to make a mixture that will be slightly wetter than most muffin batters. Stir in almonds. Spoon batter into greased muffin cups (baking papers will not work). Sprinkle additional almonds on top, if desired. Bake 20 to 25 minutes.

*Honey has twice the sweetness
as granulated sugar.*

Three-Grain Muffins

1 cup bran cereal (such as
    Bran Buds or All Bran)
$1/2$ cup cornmeal
$1/2$ cup uncooked rolled oats
$3/4$ cup boiling water
1 cup buttermilk
$1/4$ cup molasses
$1/4$ cup butter or margarine,
    melted and cooled

2 tbsp. honey
2 tbsp. applesauce
1 egg, lightly beaten
1 tsp. vanilla extract
1 cup whole wheat flour
$1^1/2$ tsp. baking soda
$1/2$ tsp. salt

Preheat oven to 375 degrees. In a large bowl stir together bran cereal, cornmeal, and oats; stir in boiling water and let stand 5 minutes. Stir in buttermilk, molasses, butter, honey, applesauce, egg, and vanilla until blended. In another large bowl stir together flour, baking soda, and salt. Make a well in center of dry ingredients; add grain-buttermilk mixture and stir just to combine. Spoon batter into greased muffin tin. Bake 20 to 25 minutes or until cake tester inserted in center of one muffin comes out clean. Remove muffin tin to wire rack. Cool 5 minutes before removing muffins from tins; finish cooling on rack. These muffins freeze well. Yield: 12 muffins

Wheat Germ Muffins

¹/₄ cup light molasses   ³/₄ cup all-purpose flour
¹/₄ cup vegetable oil   ¹/₂ tsp. salt
1 egg   2¹/₂ tsp. baking powder
1¹/₂ cups buttermilk or yogurt   ¹/₂ tsp. baking soda
1 cup whole wheat flour   ¹/₂ cup wheat germ

Topping:
1 tbsp. wheat germ

Preheat oven to 375 degrees. In large bowl beat oil and molasses together with a fork; beat in the egg and buttermilk. In separate bowl mix dry ingredients. Mix the dry ingredients into the wet ingredients. Spoon into paper-lined muffin tins. Sprinkle with 1 tbsp. wheat germ. Bake approximately 20 minutes or until golden brown.

If you don't have the desired size baking tin, make one out of heavy duty aluminum foil. Place on baking sheet in oven for support.

Wheat Germ and Molasses Muffins

3 eggs
$^1/_3$ cup brown sugar
$^2/_3$ cup vegetable oil
$^1/_4$ cup molasses
2 cups natural bran
1 cup grated carrots
1 cup applesauce or
    mashed bananas
$1^1/_2$ cups apple juice

$1^1/_2$ cups whole wheat flour
$^1/_2$ cup wheat germ
1 tsp. baking soda
2 tsp. baking powder
$^3/_4$ tsp. salt
1 tbsp. powdered milk
$^2/_3$ cup raisins or dates
$^1/_4$ cup chopped nuts
    (optional)

In large bowl beat eggs; add sugar, oil, molasses, bran, carrots, applesauce, and apple juice. Stir well. In medium bowl combine flour, wheat germ, soda, baking powder, salt, powdered milk, raisins, and nuts (if desired); mix well. Add dry ingredients all at once to egg mixture, stirring only until moistened. Bake at 375 degrees for 20 to 25 minutes. This is a very moist muffin. Yield: 24 muffins

Molasses is a byproduct of sugar manufacturing. Boil once to get light molasses. Boil twice to get dark molasses. Boil three times to get black strap, the strongest in flavor.

Wheat Germ and Raisin Muffins

$^1/_2$ cup wheat bran
1 cup buttermilk or yogurt
2 eggs
2 tbsp. olive oil
3 tbsp. molasses
$^1/_2$ cup applesauce
1 cup whole wheat flour, sifted
$^1/_4$ cup wheat germ

$^1/_4$ cup oat bran
1 tsp. baking powder
1 tsp. baking soda
$^1/_4$ tsp. ground nutmeg
$^1/_2$ tsp. cinnamon
1 tsp. grated orange rind
$^3/_4$ cup raisins

In small bowl combine the bran and buttermilk or yogurt, and mix well. Set aside. In another bowl or food processor combine the eggs, oil, molasses, and applesauce. Process to combine, then add the bran mixture and process again. In large bowl combine the flour, wheat germ, oat bran, baking powder, baking soda, nutmeg, cinnamon, and orange rind; add wet ingredients. Mix together until moistened. Fill prepared muffin tins 2/3 full. Bake at 375 degrees for 20 to 25 minutes.

Purist Oat Bran Muffins

2$\frac{1}{4}$ cups oat bran
1 tbsp. baking powder
$\frac{1}{4}$ cup raisins
$\frac{1}{4}$ cup brown sugar

2 egg whites
1$\frac{1}{4}$ cups skim milk
2 tbsp. Puritan vegetable oil
1 cup blueberries/fresh fruit

In large bowl combine oat bran, baking powder, raisins and brown sugar. In another bowl, mix egg whites, milk and oil. Stir together. Stir in blueberries. Fill to the top of paper lined muffin tins. Bake 15 to 20 minutes in preheated 425 degree oven.

Cheater Oat Bran Muffins

2$\frac{1}{4}$ cups oat bran
$\frac{3}{4}$ cup rolled oats
$\frac{1}{2}$ cup vegetable
 cup raisins
1 cup boiling water
2 eggs
2 cup skim milk
$\frac{1}{4}$ cup honey

2$\frac{1}{4}$ cups whole wheat flour
1 tbsp. sugar
1 tsp. cinnamon
2$\frac{1}{2}$ tsp. baking powder
$\frac{1}{2}$ tsp. salt
1 pint blueberries
1 cup chopped cranberries

In a large bowl, combine oat bran, oats, oil, and raisins. Add boiling water and stir. Set aside to cool. In another bowl, stir together eggs, milk and honey. Combine with oat mixture and stir well. Stir together flour, sugar, cinnamon, baking powder, and salt. Add to the oat mixture. Stir in berries. Cover with plastic wrap and let stand for 15 minutes to an hour. Fill paper lined muffin tins. Bake at 400 degrees for 20 to 25 minutes.

Bran Muffins

1 egg, lightly beaten	1 cup flour
1 cup milk	3 tsp. baking powder
2 tbsp. melted butter	$1/4$ cup sugar
1 cup bran	$1/2$ tsp. salt

Preheat oven to 375 degrees. Prepare muffin tin. Put the egg, milk, butter, and bran in a mixing bowl and let stand 10 minutes. Add the flour, baking powder, sugar and salt and stir just enough to dampen. Fill muffin cups 2/3 full. Bake for 20 minutes.

Tin coffee cans make excellent freezer containers for muffins.

Oat-Nut Muffins for Two

¹/₄ cup quick cooking
    rolled oats
2 tbsp. warm water
¹/₂ cup whole wheat flour
2 tbsp. light brown sugar
¹/₂ tsp. baking powder
¹/₄ tsp. cinnamon
¹/₄ tsp. salt
1 egg, lightly beaten

2 tbsp. vegetable oil
2 tbsp. milk
¹/₄ cup chopped nuts
2 tbsp. raisins or chopped prunes
2 tsp. whole wheat flour
1 tsp. light brown sugar
1 tsp. butter or
    margarine, softened

Combine oats and warm water in small bowl; let stand 5 minutes. Meanwhile, combine next 5 ingredients in medium mixing bowl.

Add egg and oil to oat mixture; beat to blend well. Add to dry ingredients, stirring only long enough to moisten. Fold in half of nuts and all of raisins or prunes. Place 4 paper baking cups inside 4 6-ounce glass custard cups. Divide batter evenly among these. Combine remaining ingredients in small bowl, adding reserved nuts. Toss with fork to blend. Sprinkle mixture evenly over muffin batter.

Arrange muffins on round microwave-safe platter; microwave, uncovered, on high 1 1/2 - 3 minutes, until toothpick inserted near center comes our clean. Let stand in custard cups 3 minutes before serving. Makes 4 muffins.

sweet muffins

Almond Mocha Muffins

2 tsp. instant coffee
1 tbsp. hot water
1 egg
$1/2$ cup vegetable oil
1 cup milk
$1/2$ tsp. vanilla extract
$1^1/2$ cups flour

$1/2$ cup sugar
$2^1/2$ tbsp. cocoa
1 tsp. baking powder
$1/2$ tsp. baking soda
$1/8$ tsp. salt
$2/3$ cup almonds,
    chopped or sliced

Preheat oven to 400 degrees. In large bowl dissolve coffee in hot water; add egg, oil, milk, and vanilla. Combine well. In a smaller bowl combine flour, sugar, cocoa, baking powder, baking soda, salt, almonds. Combine wet and dry mixtures; fold together gently until just mixed. Spoon batter into prepared muffin tins. Decorate top of each muffin with chopped or sliced almonds. Bake for 25 minutes. Remove from pan and cool on rack.

Always allow baked goods to cool completely before wrapping in airtight packaging for freezing.

Aloha Muffins

2 cups flour
$^1/_3$ cup sugar
2 tsp. baking powder
$^1/_8$ tsp. salt
$^3/_4$ cup roasted macadamia
    nuts, chopped
$^3/_4$ cup flaked coconut

$^1/_2$ cup dried pineapple, chopped
$^3/_4$ cup milk
$^1/_2$ cup butter or margarine,
    melted and cooled
1 egg, lightly beaten
1 tsp. vanilla extract

Preheat oven to 400 degrees. In a large bowl stir together flour, sugar, baking powder, and salt; stir in nuts, coconut, and pineapple to coat. In another bowl stir together milk, butter, egg, and vanilla until blended. Make a well in center of dry ingredients; add milk mixture and stir just to combine. Spoon batter into greased muffin tins. Bake 15 to 20 minutes or until a cake tester inserted in center of one muffin comes out clean. Remove muffin tins to wire rack. Cool 5 minutes before removing muffins from cups; finish cooling on rack. Serve warm or cool completely and store in an airtight container at room temperature. These muffins freeze well. Yield: 12 muffins

Banana 'n Chocolate Chip Muffins

$1^{1}/_{2}$ cups flour
$^{1}/_{2}$ cup sugar
2 tsp. baking powder
$^{1}/_{2}$ tsp. salt
1 egg, lightly beaten

$^{1}/_{2}$ cup milk
$^{1}/_{4}$ cup vegetable oil
$^{3}/_{4}$ cup ripe, mashed banana
$^{1}/_{2}$ cup chocolate chips
$^{1}/_{2}$ cup chopped nuts (optional)

Combine flour, sugar, baking powder, and salt. Add egg, milk, oil, and banana; stir until combined. Add chocolate chips and nuts. Spoon batter into prepared muffin tins. Bake at 400 degrees for 25 minutes. Yield: 16 muffins

Basic Muffins

2 cups flour
3 tbsp. sugar
1 tbsp. baking powder
$^{1}/_{4}$ tsp. salt

1 cup milk
$^{1}/_{4}$ cup vegetable oil
1 egg

In a large bowl combine flour, sugar, baking powder, and salt. In another bowl whisk together milk, oil, and egg. Stir wet ingredients into dry mixture; just until moist. Batter will be lumpy. Spoon batter into prepared muffin tins. Bake at 375 degrees for 15 to 20 minutes or until golden brown. Yield: 12 muffins

Butter Pecan Muffins

This batter is prepared the night before and paper liners should not be used.

$^1/_2$ cup butter, softened $^1/_2$ tsp. baking soda
1 cup brown sugar $1^1/_8$ tsp. vanilla extract
1 egg, lightly beaten   2 cups flour
1 cup milk $^2/_3$ cup chopped pecans

Grease 12 muffin cups well. Combine butter, sugar, egg, and milk until smooth. Add baking soda, vanilla, flour, and pecans. Pour into prepared muffin cups. These can be baked immediately or covered and refrigerated overnight. Heat oven to 350 degrees and bake for 15 to 20 minutes or until muffins are puffed and golden. Serve warm.

Marti's Sweet Blueberry Muffins

1 cup blueberries
4 tbsp. butter, softened
$^1/_3$ cup sugar
$^1/_2$ tsp. lemon extract

1 cup flour
1 tsp. baking powder
$^1/_2$ cup milk
2 egg whites

Preheat oven to 325 degrees. Wash the blueberries and dry on a paper towel. Beat the butter until fluffy, add the sugar and continue to beat until the mixture is light and lemon-colored. Blend in the lemon extract. In separate bowl sift together flour and baking powder. Add the dry ingredients alternately with the milk to the butter mixture. Beat the egg whites with 1/8 tsp. salt until they form stiff peaks; fold carefully into batter. Dust the blueberries with flour and stir them into batter. Fill the muffin cups 3/4 full and bake for 25 to 30 minutes. Yield: 12 muffins

Blueberries are higher in Vitamin A than most berries.

6/27/98 Didn't brown to well ~ OK - long to prepare

Butter Muffin Mix

Mix and keep for quick muffins:

5^1/$_2$ cups flour ^{1}/$_2$ cup sugar
^{1}/$_4$ cup baking powder ^{1}/$_2$ cup butter
1^1/$_2$ tsp. salt

Mix flour, baking powder, salt, and sugar. Cut in butter until mixture resembles coarse crumbs. Store in a tightly covered container in refrigerator until ready to use.

To make batter combine:

2^1/$_4$ cups Butter Muffin Mix ^{3}/$_4$ cup plus 1 tbsp. milk
1 egg

Measure muffin mix into bowl. Beat together egg and milk; add to muffin mix. Stir until moistened. Pour into paper-lined muffin tins. Bake at 425 degrees for 20 to 25 minutes.

APPLE CINNAMON: Add 3/4 cup peeled, chopped apple to batter. Sprinkle cinnamon/sugar over top of each muffin before baking.

HIDDEN JELLY CENTERS: Fill muffin cups 1/3 full. Place 1 tsp. of jelly in the center of each. Top with batter.

CRANBERRY UPSIDE DOWN MUFFINS: Combine 1/4 cup melted butter, 1/2 cup whole frozen cranberries, 1/2 cup chopped pecans, 1/4 cup firmly packed brown sugar, and 1/4 tsp. cinnamon. Heat to boiling and stir until sugar is dissolved. Spoon 1 tbsp. cranberry mixture into each muffin cup before adding batter.

Other Additions:

$1/2$ cup raisins
$1/2$ cup chopped dates
1 cup chopped dried apricots
$1/2$ cup chopped nuts
$2/3$ cup blueberries and
    2 tbsp. sugar
$1/2$ cup coconut and $1/2$ cup
    dried pineapple, chopped

1 cup chocolate, butterscotch
    or peanut butter chips
1 cup M & M's
1 cup chopped prunes
1 tsp. almond extract and
    1 cup slivered almonds
1 cup chopped caramels

To avoid illness keep countertops and utensils sanitary by washing often with antibacterial cleansers.

Black Forest Muffins

6 squares (1 oz. each)
    semisweet chocolate
$^1/_4$ cup butter or margarine
$^1/_2$ cup buttermilk
$^1/_2$ cup sugar
1 egg, lightly beaten
2 tbsp. brandy or
    cherry-flavored brandy

1 tsp. vanilla extract
1 cup dark sweet
    cherries, chopped
$1^3/_4$ cup flour
1 tsp. baking soda
$^1/_4$ tsp. salt

Preheat oven to 400 degrees. In a small saucepan melt chocolate with butter over low heat. Let stand 10 minutes or until cooled. In a small bowl stir chocolate mixture with buttermilk, sugar, egg, brandy, and vanilla until blended; stir in cherries. In a large bowl stir together flour, baking soda, and salt. Make a well in center of dry ingredients; add chocolate mixture and stir just to combine. Spoon batter into prepared muffin cups; bake 20 to 25 minutes or until a cake tester inserted in center of one muffin comes out clean. Remove muffin tin to wire rack. Cool 5 minutes before removing muffins from cups; finish cooling on rack. Serve warm or cool completely and store in an airtight container at room temperature. These muffins freeze well. Yield: 12 muffins

Before melting chocolate, rub the inside of the pan or bowl with butter. The chocolate will not stick.

Cappuccino Muffins

2 cups flour
$^3/_4$ cup sugar
$2^1/_2$ tsp. baking powder
2 tsp. instant
    cappuccino powder
$^1/_4$ tsp. salt
$^3/_4$ tsp. ground cinnamon

1 cup milk
$^1/_2$ cup butter or margarine,
    melted and cooled
1 egg, lightly beaten
$1^1/_4$ tsp. vanilla extract
$^1/_2$ cup semisweet chocolate chips

Preheat oven to 375 degrees. In a large bowl stir together flour, sugar, baking powder, cappuccino powder, salt, and cinnamon. In another bowl, stir together milk, butter, egg, and vanilla until blended. Make a well in center of dry ingredients; add milk mixture and stir just to combine. Stir in chips. Spoon batter into prepared muffin tins. Bake 15 to 20 minutes or until a cake tester inserted in center of one muffin comes out clean. Remove muffin tins to wire rack. Cool 5 minutes before removing muffins from cups; finish cooling on rack. Serve warm or cool completely and store in an airtight container at room temperature. These muffins freeze well. Yield: 10-12 muffins

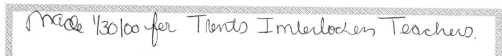

Made 1/30/00 for Trents Imterlochen Teachers.

Coffee Almond Muffins

1 tbsp. instant coffee	1^1/$_2$ cups flour
^{1}/$_2$ cup hot water	3 tsp. baking powder
^{1}/$_2$ cup whole milk or cream	^{1}/$_3$ cup sugar
1 egg, beaten	^{3}/$_4$ tsp. salt
^{1}/$_2$ cup vegetable oil	^{1}/$_2$ cups chopped almonds

In mixing bowl dissolve coffee in hot water and add the cream, beaten egg, and vegetable oil. In a large bowl mix together flour, baking powder, salt, and sugar; stir in almonds. Pour liquid ingredients into the dry mixture only to moisten. Spoon batter into greased muffin tins. Bake at 375 degrees for 15 to 20 minutes.

Chocolate Cheesecake Muffins

1 pkg. (3 oz.) cream cheese	2 tbsp. baking powder
2 tbsp. sugar	^{1}/$_2$ tbsp. salt
1 cup flour	1 egg, lightly beaten
^{1}/$_2$ cup sugar	^{3}/$_4$ cup milk
3 tbsp. cocoa powder	^{1}/$_3$ cup vegetable oil

In a small bowl beat cream cheese and 2 tbsp. sugar until light and fluffy; set aside. In a large bowl stir together flour, 1/2 cup sugar, cocoa, baking powder, and salt. In another bowl combine egg, milk, and oil. Make a well in center of dry ingredients; add egg mixture all at once to dry ingredients; stir until moistened. Spoon 2 tbsp. of the chocolate batter into paper lined muffin tins. Drop 1 tsp. cream cheese on top and then more chocolate batter. Bake at 350 degrees for 20 minutes.

Chocolate Chip Muffins

2 cups flour
3 tsp. baking powder
$^1/_2$ tsp. salt
2 tbsp. sugar

1 egg, lightly beaten
1 cup milk
$^1/_4$ cup butter, melted
$^1/_2$ cup mini chocolate chips

Preheat oven to 350 degrees. Mix dry ingredients together. Add the egg, milk, and butter; stirring only enough to dampen the flour. Add chocolate chips to batter. Batter will be lumpy. Fill paper-lined muffin tins 2/3 full. Bake for 20 to 25 minutes.

Sylvia's Double Chocolate Muffins
(for the true chocolate lover)

2 oz. unsweetened chocolate
$^1/_2$ cup margarine
1 cup flour
1 tsp. baking powder
$^1/_4$ tsp. baking soda
2 eggs

1 cup applesauce
$^3/_4$ cup sugar
$1^1/_2$ tsp. vanilla extract
1 cup semi-sweet chocolate chips
confectioner's sugar

In small saucepan melt the unsweetened chocolate and margarine; set aside to cool. In a large bowl combine flour, baking powder, and baking soda. In a medium bowl whisk eggs, applesauce, sugar, vanilla, and cooled chocolate mixture. Pour wet ingredients into dry mixture; stir just until moistened. Stir in chocolate chips. Fill greased muffin tins with batter. Bake at 375 degrees for 15 minutes. Yield: 12-15 muffins

Chocolate Orange Muffins

2 medium oranges, scrubbed
3 oz. bittersweet chocolate
1 cup sugar
$1/2$ cup butter, softened
2 eggs

$1/3$ cup orange juice
$1/2$ cup plain yogurt
2 cups flour
1 tsp. baking powder
$1/2$ tsp. baking soda

Grate orange peel; set aside. Chop chocolate into small pieces; set aside. In a bowl beat sugar and butter together. Add eggs, orange peel, orange juice, and yogurt; mix well. In a small bowl combine flour, baking powder, and baking soda; add this mixture to liquid ingredients. Stir in chocolate pieces. Bake at 375 degrees for 20 to 25 minutes.

Cinnamon Raisin Muffins

$1^1/2$ cups whole wheat flour
$1/3$ cup firmly packed
   brown sugar
3 tsp. baking powder
$1/2$ tsp. salt
1 tsp. cinnamon

$1/2$ cup wheat germ
$3/4$ cup raisins
$2/3$ cup milk
$1/3$ cup vegetable oil
2 eggs

In large bowl combine first seven ingredients; mix well. Add remaining ingredients. Spoon batter into prepared muffin tins. Bake at 400 degrees for 20 minutes.

Cinnamon Applesauce Muffins

1 cup flour
3 tsp. baking powder
$^3/_4$ tsp. cinnamon
$^1/_4$ tsp. salt
$^1/_8$ tsp. nutmeg
$^3/_4$ cup rolled oats

$^1/_4$ cup brown sugar
1 egg
$^1/_4$ cup vegetable oil
$^1/_3$ cup milk
$^2/_3$ cup applesauce

In large bowl mix dry ingredients together with a fork. In a separate bowl beat egg; then add oil and milk. Stir in applesauce. Add the wet mixture into dry ingredients, mixing only until moistened. Spoon into greased muffin tins. Bake at 375 degrees for 20 minutes.

Cinnamon is the bark of the Laurel Tree, native to China and Indonesia.

Made w/ Rachee in 2013 of 98. R & N liked. Trent-OK

Cherry Amaretto Muffins

Make these for very special occasions – they delight the eye and the palate. The alcohol evaporates in the heat, leaving only the lovely Amaretto flavor in every bite.

1/2 cup chopped pitted cherries
1/4 cup Amaretto liqueur
2 eggs
2 tbsp. vegetable oil
3 tbsp. honey
1/4 tsp. almond extract
3/4 cup apple or orange juice
2 tbsp. Amaretto liqueur

1 1/2 cups sifted whole
    wheat pastry flour
2 tbsp. wheat germ
2 tbsp. oat bran
2 tbsp. lecithin granules
1 tsp. baking powder
1 tsp. baking soda
1/2 cups chopped almonds

In a small bowl combine the cherries and Amaretto. Set aside. In a mixing bowl or food processor blend the eggs, oil, honey, almond extract, fruit juice, and two tbsp. of additional Amaretto. Stir in the cherry mixture. In another bowl combine the pastry flour, wheat germ, oat bran, lecithin granules, baking powder, and baking soda. Preheat oven to 400 degrees. Prepare muffin tins. Add the dry ingredients to the cherry mixture and blend just enough to moisten the pastry flour mixture. Stir in the chopped almonds. Bake 15-20 minutes or until done.

Spiced Cherry Muffins

$1^1/_4$ cup dried cherries
hot water
1 package (18 oz.)
    spice cake mix
1 egg, lightly beaten

1 cup water
$^1/_3$ cup vegetable oil
1 tsp. baking powder
$^3/_4$ cup chopped walnuts
1 container (8 oz.) sour cream

Place cherries into a medium bowl; cover with hot water. Set aside. In a large bowl combine cake mix, egg, 1 cup water, oil, and baking powder; stir until ingredients are moistened. Do not over mix. Drain water from cherries; fold cherries and walnuts into cake mixture. Spoon a tablespoon of batter into greased muffin cups. Spoon a rounded teaspoon of sour cream on top of the batter in each cup. Fill cups with remaining batter, about 2/3 full. Bake in a pre-heated 350 degree oven for 20 minutes. Yield: 18 muffins

Sour cream can be home made by adding 3-4 drops of pure lemon juice to every 3/4 cup of whipping cream. Let stand at room temperature for 30-40 minutes.

Cranberry Nut Muffins

$1/2$ cup margarine or
    butter, softened
$3/4$ cup sugar
2 eggs
2 cups flour
$2^3/4$ tsp. baking powder

1 tsp. cinnamon
$1/2$ tsp. salt
1 can (16 oz.) whole
    cranberry sauce
1 cup chopped walnuts

Heat oven to 350 degrees. Grease muffin tins or line with baking papers. In medium sized bowl, beat margarine until creamy. Beat in sugar until pale and fluffy. Add eggs one at a time. In a small bowl mix flour, baking powder, cinnamon, and salt. Stir into margarine mixture. Fold in cranberry sauce and walnuts. Spoon batter into muffin tins. Bake for 15 minutes or until toothpick inserted in center of one muffin comes out clean.

Chocolate Buttermilk Muffins

$1^3/4$ cup flour
$1/3$ cup cocoa powder
$1/2$ cup sugar
$1^1/2$ tsp. baking powder
$1/2$ tsp. baking soda

1 egg
2 tbsp. vegetable oil
$1^1/4$ cup buttermilk
$1^1/2$ tsp. vanilla extract

In a large bowl combine dry ingredients. In a smaller bowl whisk together egg, oil, buttermilk, and vanilla. Pour wet ingredients into dry mixture; stir just until moistened. Spoon batter into greased muffin cups. Bake at 400 degrees for 15 to 20 minutes. Yield: 12 muffins

Simple Crumbcake Muffins

1³/₄ cups flour
³/₄ cup sugar
1³/₄ tsp. baking powder
¹/₄ tsp. salt
1 cup milk
¹/₂ cup butter or margarine,
    melted and cooled

1 egg, plus 1 egg yolk,
    lightly beaten
1¹/₄ tsp. vanilla extract
3 tbsp. confectioners sugar

Topping:
1 cup flour
¹/₃ cup butter or
    margarine, softened

¹/₃ cup firmly packed brown sugar
¹/₈ tsp. cinnamon
¹/₈ tsp. nutmeg

Preheat oven to 400 degrees. In a small bowl stir together topping ingredients until mixture resembles coarse crumbs; set topping aside. In a large bowl stir together flour, sugar, baking powder, and salt. In a smaller bowl whisk together milk, butter, egg, vanilla & confectioners sugar. Pour wet ingredients into dry mixture; stir just until moistened. Spoon batter into greased muffin cups. Bake at 375 degrees for 15-20 minutes. Top with topping mixture while still warm.

Some people collect nutmeg grinders as a hobby. There are literally hundreds of varieties.

103

Dorothy's Dunking Muffins

They taste like donuts!

1³/₄ cup flour
1¹/₂ tsp. baking powder
¹/₂ tsp. salt
¹/₂ tsp. nutmeg
¹/₄ tsp. cinnamon
¹/₃ cup vegetable oil

³/₄ cup sugar (first amount)
1 egg
³/₄ cup milk
¹/₂ cup butter, melted
³/₄ cup sugar (second amount)
1 tsp. cinnamon

In a bowl combine flour, baking powder, salt, nutmeg, and cinnamon. In another bowl thoroughly combine oil, sugar, egg, and milk. Add liquid ingredients to dry mixture; stir only to combine. Bake at 350 degrees for 20 to 25 minutes. (In small bowl mix sugar and cinnamon together.) Shake muffins out immediately while hot and dip in melted butter, then sugar and cinnamon.

Double Fudge Muffins

5 oz. semi-sweet
   chocolate chips
2 oz. unsweetened
   chocolate, chopped
$1/3$ cup butter
$3/4$ cup sour cream
$2/3$ cup brown sugar

$1/4$ light corn syrup
1 egg, room temperature
$1^1/2$ tsp. vanilla
$1^1/2$ cups flour
1 tsp. baking soda
$1/2$ tsp. salt
1 cup chocolate chips

Melt first 3 ingredients, stirring until smooth; cool slightly. Whisk sour cream, brown sugar, corn syrup, egg, and vanilla into chocolate mixture. Combine flour, baking soda, and salt in a large bowl; stir in chocolate chips. Make a well in the center of the dry ingredients. Pour chocolate mixture into well; stir until blended (batter will be lumpy). Fill paper-lined muffin tins 3/4 full. Bake at 400 degrees for 20 minutes or until a toothpick inserted in center of one muffin comes out clean.

Reminder... never taste the batter when baking. It may contain raw eggs and salmonella contamination.

Gina's Gingerbread Muffins

1¼ cups all-purpose flour
½ cup whole wheat flour
½ firmly packed brown sugar
2 tsp. ground ginger
1 tsp. baking soda
⅛ tsp. salt
¾ tsp. ground cinnamon

⅛ tsp. ground cloves
¼ tsp. ground nutmeg
¾ cup buttermilk
½ cup canola oil
2 eggs, lightly beaten
¼ cup molasses
1 cup raisins or currants

Preheat oven to 400 degrees. In a large bowl stir together flours, brown sugar, ginger, baking soda, salt, cinnamon, cloves, and nutmeg. In another bowl stir together buttermilk, oil, eggs, and molasses until blended. Make a well in center of dry ingredients; add buttermilk mixture and stir just to combine. Stir in raisins. Spoon batter into prepared muffin tins. Bake 15 to 20 minutes or until a cake tester inserted in center of one muffin comes out clean. Remove muffin tins to wire rack. Cool 5 minutes before removing muffins from cups; finish cooling on rack. Serve warm or cool completely and store in an airtight container at room temperature. These muffins freeze well. Yield: 12 muffins

It has been said that though the Egyptians were eating gingerbread when the great pyramid of Cheops was young, the first recipe originated from Greece, where it was discovered by a baker on the island of Rhodes, about 2,400 B.C.

Peanut Butter Fudge Filled Muffins
(a true heavenly vision)

$^1/_2$ cup semi-sweet
   chocolate chips
1 tbsp. butter or margarine
$1^2/_3$ cups flour
$^1/_2$ cup firmly packed
   brown sugar
1 tbsp. baking powder
$^1/_8$ tsp. salt

$^3/_4$ cup milk
$^1/_2$ cup peanut butter
$^1/_3$ cup vegetable oil
1 egg, lightly beaten
1 tsp. vanilla extract
$^1/_3$ cup chopped salted peanuts
   without skins (optional)

Preheat oven to 400 degrees. In a small saucepan heat chocolate chips and butter until melted, stirring constantly; remove from heat and reserve. In a large bowl stir together flour, brown sugar, baking powder, and salt. In another bowl stir together milk, peanut butter, oil, egg, and vanilla until blended. Make a well in center of dry ingredients; add milk mixture and stir just to combine. Spoon half of batter into nine greased (3 1/2- to 4-ounce) muffin cups. Divide chocolate mixture among muffin cups, scant teaspoon per cup; do not let filling touch sides of cup. Spoon remaining batter into cups over filling. Sprinkle tops of muffins with chopped peanuts, if desired. Bake 20 to 25 minutes or until lightly browned. Remove muffin tins to wire rack. Cool 5 minutes before removing muffins from cups; finishing cooling on rack. Serve warm or cool completely and store in an airtight container at room temperature. Yield: 9 muffins

Moist & Delicious Hazelnut Muffins

2 cups flour
$^1/_2$ cup sugar
$1^1/_2$ tsp. baking powder
$^1/_2$ tsp. baking soda
$^1/_2$ tsp. salt
$^1/_2$ cup buttermilk
$^1/_2$ cup hazelnut-flavored
    liqueur

$^1/_3$ cup butter or margarine,
    melted and cooled
1 egg, lightly beaten
$^3/_4$ cup chopped
    hazelnuts (filberts)
$^1/_2$ cup coconut

Preheat oven to 400 degrees. In a large bowl stir together flour, sugar, baking powder, baking soda, and salt. In another bowl stir together buttermilk, hazelnut-flavored liqueur, butter, and egg until blended. Make a well in center of dry ingredients; add buttermilk mixture and stir just to combine. Stir in hazelnuts. Spoon batter into prepared muffin cups. Bake 15 to 20 minutes or until a cake tester inserted in center of one muffin comes out clean. Remove muffin tins to wire rack. Cool 5 minutes before removing muffins from cups; finish cooling on rack. Serve warm or cool completely and store in an airtight container at room temperature. Yield: 12 muffins

Jelly Muffins

1³/₄ cups flour
¹/₄ cup sugar
2 tsp. baking powder
¹/₂ tsp. salt

1 egg, lightly beaten
³/₄ cup milk
¹/₃ cup vegetable oil
assorted jelly or jam

In a large mixing bowl stir together flour, sugar, baking powder, and salt. Make a well in the center. In another bowl combine egg, milk, and oil; stir together. Add egg mixture all at once to flour mixture. Stir just until moistened; batter will be lumpy. Fill paper-lined muffin cups 2/3 full. Spoon 1 tsp. jelly atop batter in each muffin cup before baking. Bake at 400 degrees for 20 to 25 minutes. Yield: 10-12 muffins

Tangy Lemonade Muffins

1¹/₂ cups flour
¹/₄ sugar
2¹/₂ tsp. baking powder
¹/₄ tsp. salt
1 egg, lightly beaten

1 can (6 oz.) frozen
   lemonade, thawed
¹/₄ cup milk
¹/₃ cup vegetable oil

In a large bowl mix together dry ingredients. In another bowl combine egg, 1/2 cup of the lemonade, milk, and oil. Add to dry ingredients; stir just until moistened. Fill greased muffin cups. Bake at 375 degrees for 15-20 minutes or until done. While hot, brush with remaining lemonade and sprinkle with sugar.

Took to Dell at '99 Craft Fair ~Interlochen School

Lemon Yogurt Muffins

2 cups flour
2$^1/_2$ tsp. baking powder
$^1/_2$ tsp. baking soda
$^1/_4$ tsp. salt
1 tbsp. grated lemon peel

1 egg, beaten
$^1/_4$ cup vegetable oil
$^1/_3$ cup honey
1 carton (8 oz.) lowfat
    lemon yogurt

Preheat oven to 400 degrees. In a large bowl stir together flour, baking powder, baking soda, salt, and grated lemon peel. In a separate bowl combine egg, oil, honey, and yogurt; mix together well. Add this mixture to dry ingredients. Stir just until moistened. Fill greased or paper-line muffin cups 2/3 full. Bake for 18 minutes or until golden brown. Yield: 12 muffins

NOTE: Be creative and use your favorite flavor of yogurt.

Maple Pecan Muffins

1 1/2 cups whole wheat flour
1 1/2 tsp. baking powder
1/2 tsp. salt
1/2 cup chopped pecans
1/3 cup maple syrup

2 tbsp. vegetable oil
1 egg
2/3 cup water
1 tsp. vanilla extract

Preheat oven to 375 degrees. Sift flour, baking powder, and salt together. Stir in nuts. In a large bowl beat maple syrup and oil together; add the egg. Add water, vanilla, and the dry ingredients, stirring just enough to mix. Spoon into prepared muffin tin. Bake 12 to 15 minutes.

Maple and Walnut Muffins

2 eggs, beaten
3 tbsp. walnut oil or
   unsalted butter, softened
$1/4$ cup maple syrup
$1/2$ cup milk
$1/2$ cup whole wheat pastry flour

$1/4$ cup wheat germ
$1/4$ cup oat bran
2 tsp. baking powder
1 tsp. baking soda
$1/3$ cup chopped walnuts

In a bowl mix together the eggs, oil or butter, maple syrup, and milk. In another bowl combine the pastry flour, wheat germ, bran, baking powder, and baking soda; mix well. Stir in the nuts. Preheat oven to 350 degrees. Spoon batter into prepared muffin tins. Bake for 20 to 25 minutes or until brown. Yield: 12 muffins

Rich Delicious Orange Tea Muffins

$1^1/2$ cups flour
$1/2$ cup sugar
2 tsp. baking powder
$1/2$ tsp. salt

$1/2$ cup butter
$1/2$ cup orange juice
2 eggs
grated rind of one orange

In a large bowl combine flour, sugar, baking powder, and salt. In a saucepan melt butter; set aside. Blend orange juice, orange rind, and eggs; add to butter. Stir liquid ingredients into dry mixture. Spoon batter into paper-lined muffin tins. For each muffin, soak 1 sugar cube in a small amount of orange juice and place on top of batter. Bake at 350 degrees for 15 to 20 minutes.

Glazed Maple Syrup Muffins

$1/4$ cup margarine or
    butter, softened
$1/2$ cup sugar
$3/4$ tsp. salt
$1^1/4$ cup flour

2 tsp. baking powder
$3/4$ cup rolled oats
$1/2$ cup milk
$1/2$ cup maple syrup
$1/2$ cup chopped pecans (optional)

Glaze:

1 tbsp. butter
$1/2$ cup confectioners sugar

1 tbsp. maple syrup

Blend together margarine or butter, sugar, and salt. Add dry ingredients and blend with pastry cutter until mixture is crumbly. Mix in oats. Blend milk and syrup together in a measuring cup; pour over dry ingredients, stirring only to moisten. Bake at 350 degrees for 20 minutes. Spread glaze over muffins when slightly cooled.

Sweet Orange Muffins

2 cups flour
¹/₂ cup sugar
1 tbsp. baking powder
¹/₄ tsp. salt

¹/₄ cup vegetable oil
1 egg, lightly beaten
¹/₂ cup orange juice
¹/₂ cup orange marmalade

Topping:
¹/₄ cup sugar
1¹/₂ tbsp. flour
¹/₂ tsp. cinnamon

¹/₄ tsp. nutmeg
1 tbsp. butter or
   margarine, softened

In a large bowl combine dry ingredients. In a smaller bowl combine egg, oil, orange juice, and marmalade. Stir egg mixture into dry ingredients just until moistened. Fill greased muffin tins 3/4 full. Combine topping ingredients and sprinkle on muffins before baking. Bake at 375 degrees for 15 to 20 minutes. Yield: 12 muffins

Orange Streusel Muffins

1³/₄ cups flour
¹/₄ cup sugar
2¹/₂ tsp. baking powder
¹/₂ tsp. salt

1 egg, lightly beaten
³/₄ cup milk
¹/₃ cup vegetable oil
¹/₄ cup orange marmalade

Streusel Topping:
2 tbsp. flour
2 tbsp. brown sugar
1 tbsp. butter, softened

1 tsp. cinnamon
3 tbsp. chopped pecans

Preheat oven to 400 degrees. In a small bowl mix together streusel top-ping ingredients; set aside. In a medium bowl mix flour, sugar, baking powder, and salt; make a well in the center. In a small bowl combine egg, milk, and oil. Add egg mixture all at once to flour mixture, stirring until moistened. Batter will be slightly lumpy. Spoon 1 tbsp. of batter into each paper-lined muffin cup. Top each with 1 tsp. marmalade. Spoon another tbsp. of the batter atop the marmalade. Sprinkle with streusel topping. Bake for 20 to 25 minutes. Yield: 12 muffins.

Basic Muffin Mix

Mix and keep for quick muffins:

5$^{1}/_{2}$ cups flour $^{1}/_{2}$ cup sugar
$^{1}/_{4}$ cup baking powder $^{1}/_{2}$ cup butter
1$^{1}/_{2}$ tsp. salt

Mix flour, baking powder, salt, and sugar. Cut in butter until mixture resembles coarse crumbs. Store in a tightly covered container in refrigerator until ready to use.

To make batter combine:

2$^{1}/_{4}$ cups Basic Muffin Mix $^{3}/_{4}$ cup plus 1 tbsp. milk
1 egg

Measure muffin mix into bowl. Beat together egg and milk; add to muffin mix. Stir until moistened. Pour into paper-lined muffin tins. Bake at 425 degrees for 20 to 25 minutes.

PECAN MUFFINS: Use 1/4 cup sugar. Add 1/2 cup chopped pecans to the batter. After filling the cups, sprinkle with sugar, cinnamon, and more chopped nuts.

Peach Upside-Down Muffins

2 cups cake flour
1/2 cup sugar
3 tsp. baking powder
1/4 tsp. salt
1/4 cup vegetable oil

2 eggs
1 cup milk
butter or margarine
brown sugar, lightly packed
cooked, dried, peach halves

Sift together flour, sugar, baking powder, and salt three times; add the vegetable oil, eggs, and milk. Beat until batter is smooth and light. Place 1 tsp. butter and 1 tbsp. brown sugar in each muffin cup; heat until melted and thoroughly blended. Cut peach halves in 3 sections to resemble petals; place in muffin cups with cut-side up. fill cups half full of batter. Bake at 375 degrees for 25 minutes.

Peanut Butter and Jelly Muffins

1 cup whole wheat flour
1 1/2 tbsp. baking powder
1/2 cup peanut butter
2 eggs
1/4 cup honey

3/4 cup milk
1/2 cup blueberries
jam
nutmeg

In a large bowl mix flour and baking powder. In another bowl mix peanut butter, eggs, honey, and milk; add to flour mixture. Stir in blueberries. Spoon batter into paper-lined muffin tins. Swirl 1 tbsp. jam into each muffin. Sprinkle the muffins with nutmeg. Bake at 375 degrees for 20 minutes.

Southern Peanut Butter Muffins

1 cup flour
1 tbsp. baking powder
$^1/_2$ tsp. salt
$^1/_2$ cup peanut butter

2 tbsp. honey
1 egg, beaten
$^2/_3$ cup milk

In a bowl blend together all the dry ingredients. In another bowl blend together the remaining ingredients; pour mixture into dry ingredients and blend well. Pour batter into muffin pans, fill 2/3 full. Bake at 425 degrees for 12 to 15 minutes.

Piña Colada Muffins

$^1/_2$ cup sugar
1 egg
$^1/_4$ cup butter
1 cup sour cream
1 tsp. rum extract
$1^1/_2$ cups flour

1 tsp. baking powder
$^1/_2$ tsp. baking soda
$^1/_4$ tsp. salt
1 small can crushed
    pineapple, drained
$^1/_2$ cup coconut

In a medium bowl combine sugar, egg, butter, sour cream, and rum extract. In a large bowl stir together dry ingredients; add pineapple, coconut, and wet ingredients. Bake at 375 degrees for 20 minutes.

Poppy Seed Muffins

3 cups flour
2$^1/_2$ cups sugar
1$^1/_2$ tsp. baking powder
1$^1/_2$ tsp. salt
1$^1/_2$ cups vegetable oil

1$^1/_2$ cups milk
3 eggs
1$^1/_2$ tsp. almond extract
1$^1/_2$ tbsp. poppy seeds

Preheat oven to 350 degrees. Line muffin cups with papers. Combine flour, sugar, baking powder, and salt in large bowl. Whisk oil, milk, eggs, and almond extract in another bowl. Mix together until moistened. Stir in poppy seeds. Bake for 30 minutes or until golden brown. Yield: 24 muffins

Poppy Seed & Orange Muffins

1 egg
2 tbsp. frozen orange juice
    concentrate, slightly thawed
2 tbsp. honey
2 tbsp. butter, softened
$^1/_2$ cup yogurt or buttermilk
2 tbsp. wheat bran
$^1/_3$ cup unsweetened
    orange marmalade

1$^1/_2$ cups sifted whole
    wheat pastry flour
3 tbsp. poppy seeds
2 tbsp. lecithin granules
2 tbsp. wheat germ
2 tbsp. oat bran
1 tbsp. grated orange rind
1 tsp. baking powder
1 tsp. baking soda

Orange Glaze:
2 tbsp. orange marmalade

1 tbsp. boiling water

In a mixing bowl or food processor blend together the egg, orange concentrate, honey, butter, yogurt or buttermilk, bran, and marmalade. In another bowl mix together the flour, seeds, lecithin granules, wheat germ, oat bran, orange rind, baking powder, and baking soda. Preheat oven to 400 degrees. Grease 12 muffin cups.

Linda's Lemon Poppy Seed Muffins

$1/4$ cup poppy seeds	2 tsp. baking powder
3 tbsp. honey	$1/4$ tsp. salt
2 tbsp. water	$1/2$ cup vegetable oil
3 tbsp. lemon juice	2 eggs
$1^3/4$ cup flour	2 tbsp. grated lemon peel
$3/4$ cup sugar	$3/4$ cup fat-free sour cream
1 tsp. baking soda	

In a small saucepan combine poppy seeds, honey, and water. Place over low heat. Cook for approximately 5 minutes, stirring frequently, until seeds are moistened and mixture resembles wet sand. Let mixture cool, then stir in lemon juice. In a large bowl combine flour, baking soda, baking powder, and salt. In a smaller bowl mix oil, sugar, eggs, lemon peel, sour cream, and poppy seed mixture. Pour wet ingredients into dry mixture; stir just until moist. Fill greased muffin cups 3/4 full. Bake at 375 degrees for 18 to 20 minutes or until golden brown. Yield: 12-18 muffins

Almond Poppy Seed Muffins

$^2/_3$ cup milk
$^1/_3$ cup poppy seeds
$1^1/_2$ cup flour
2 tsp. baking powder
$^1/_2$ tsp. baking soda
$^1/_8$ tsp. salt

$^1/_2$ cup butter, softened
1 cup sugar
2 eggs, beaten
$^3/_4$ tsp. almond extract
$^3/_4$ cup sliced almonds

Heat milk to scalding and pour over poppy seeds; set aside to cool. In a large bowl combine flour, sugar, baking powder, baking soda, and salt. In a medium bowl cream sugar and butter; then add eggs, almond extract, and milk mixture. Pour wet ingredients into dry mixture, stir just until moist. Stir 1/2 cup sliced almonds into mixture. Divide batter into greased muffin cups, evenly divide and sprinkle the remaining sliced almonds over the prepared batter. Bake at 375 degrees for 20 minutes. Yield: 12 muffins

Poundcake Muffins

$1^3/_4$ cup flour
$^1/_4$ tsp. salt
$^1/_4$ tsp. baking soda
1 cup sugar
$^1/_2$ cup butter or
    margarine, softened

$^1/_2$ cup sour cream
1 tsp. vanilla
$^1/_2$ tsp. lemon or vanilla extract
2 eggs, lightly beaten

Preheat oven to 400 degrees. In a small bowl stir together flour, salt, and baking soda. In a large bowl beat sugar and butter with electric mixer until well combined. Beat in sour cream and extract until well blended. Beat in eggs one at a time, until well blended. Beat in dry ingredients until combined. Spoon batter into greased muffin tins. Bake 20 to 25 minutes or until a cake tester inserted in center of one muffin comes out clean. Yield: 9 muffins

Glazed Pumpkin Muffins

1¼ cups all-purpose flour
1 cup whole wheat flour
1 cup sugar
1 tsp. baking powder
1 tsp. baking soda
2 eggs

1 cup canned solid
    pack pumpkin
1 tsp. salt
1 cup. butter, softened
1 tsp. pumpkin pie spice

Glaze:
1 egg yolk

¼ cup whipping cream

Preheat oven to 350 degrees. In a large bowl mix flours, sugar, baking powder, and soda. Combine eggs, pumpkin, and salt in another bowl. Add to dry ingredients; mix until smooth. Stir in butter and pumpkin pie spice. Pour into paper-lined muffin tins. Brush with glaze. Bake 45 minutes.

Sweet Plum Muffins

1 cup finely chopped plums
2^1/$_2$ cups flour
2 tsp. baking soda
^{1}/$_4$ tsp. salt
1 cup sugar
^{1}/$_4$ cup butter or
    margarine, melted

2 eggs, lightly beaten
^{1}/$_2$ cup milk
^{1}/$_2$ cup chopped
    walnuts (optional)
2 tbsp. sugar

Sprinkle plums with 1 tbsp. flour and toss lightly. In a large bowl combine flour, baking soda, and salt with 1 cup sugar. In another bowl mix the melted butter, eggs, and milk; stirring until smooth. Add the liquid ingredients to the dry ones. Stir just until mixture is moistened. Fold in plums and walnuts. Spoon batter into greased muffin tins, filling about 2/3 full. Sprinkle sugar on top of batter. Bake at 400 degrees for 20 to 25 minutes. Yield: 12-18 muffins

Keep nuts refrigerated and they will stay fresh longer.

Raisin Rum Muffins

1 egg
$1/3$ cup sugar
$1/2$ cup butter or
    margarine, melted
$1/2$ cup milk
$1/4$ cup light rum
1 tsp. vanilla extract

$1/2$ cup raisins
$1^3/4$ cup cake flour
$1^1/2$ tsp. baking powder
$1/2$ tsp. baking soda
$1/2$ tsp. salt
$1/4$ tsp. ground nutmeg
$1/8$ tsp. cinnamon

In a large bowl combine egg, sugar, butter, milk, rum, vanilla, and raisins; mix well. In a separate bowl combine cake flour, baking powder, baking soda, salt, nutmeg, and cinnamon; mix well. Add dry ingredients to wet mixture; fold together gently until just mixed. Spoon into prepared muffin tins. Bake at 400 degrees for 20 minutes. Remove from pan and cool on rack.

Variation:

RUM 'N EGGNOG: Substitute 1/2 cup commercial or homemade eggnog for milk or dissolve 3 tbsp. eggnog crystals in 1/2 cup milk.

HINT: You may substitute 1 tsp. rum extract for vanilla, omit rum liquor and change milk to 3/4 cup.

Maris' Sweet Potato Pie Muffins

2 eggs
$^1/_3$ cup maple syrup
2 tbsp. butter or margarine
$^1/_2$ cup crushed, unsweetened
    pineapple with juice
1 tsp. vanilla extract
1 cup raw sweet potato, grated
$^1/_2$ cup raisins, plumped

$^1/_2$ cup chopped walnuts
    (optional)
$1^3/_4$ cup sifted whole wheat flour
$^1/_4$ cup wheat germ
2 tsp. baking powder
1 tsp. cinnamon
$^1/_8$ tsp. ground nutmeg

In a large bowl or food processor blend together the eggs, maple syrup, butter, pineapple, vanilla, sweet potato, raisins, and walnuts (if desired). In another bowl stir together the wheat flour, wheat germ, baking powder, cinnamon, and nutmeg.

Muffin Shortcakes

2 cups flour
3 tsp. sugar
3 tsp. baking powder

$^1/_4$ tsp. salt
$^1/_2$ cup shortening
$^3/_4$ cup milk

In a large bowl combine first four ingredients; add shortening. Stir mixture with fork or pastry cutter until mixture is crumbly. Pour in milk; stir with fork 20 to 30 strokes. Fill greased muffin cups with batter. Bake at 400 degrees for 18 to 20 minutes or until tops are light brown. Yield: 6 muffins

SERVING SUGGESTION: Top warm muffins with strawberries, peaches or raspberries.

Chocolate Whiskey Muffins

³/₄ cup flour
¹/₂ tsp. baking soda
¹/₄ tsp. salt
¹/₂ cup butter or
    margarine, softened
¹/₂ cup sugar
1 square (1 oz.) semisweet
    chocolate, melted

1 egg, lightly beaten
1 tbsp. whiskey
³/₄ tsp. vanilla or almond extract
²/₃ cup semisweet chocolate chips
¹/₂ cup chopped almonds
    (optional)

Preheat oven to 400 degrees. In a medium bowl stir together flour, baking soda, and salt. In a large bowl cream butter and sugar together until light and fluffy; beat in chocolate, egg, whiskey, and extract. Add dry ingredients and beat just to combine; stir in chips and almonds. Spoon batter into prepared muffin tins. Bake 15 to 20 minutes or until a cake tester inserted in center of one muffin comes out clean. Remove muffin tins to wire rack. Cool 5 minutes before removing muffins from cups; finish cooling rack. Serve warm or cool completely and store in an airtight container at room temperature. These muffins freeze well. Yield: 9 muffins

Yogurt Muffins

1 cup all-purpose flour
$^1/_2$ cup whole wheat flour
$^3/_4$ cup sugar (or preserves)
2 tsp. baking powder
1 tsp. baking soda

$^1/_2$ tsp. salt
$^2/_3$ cup plain yogurt
$^2/_3$ cup skim milk
$^1/_2$ cup fruit (berries,
    grated apples, etc.)

In large bowl mix all ingredients together. Spoon batter into prepared muffin tins. Bake at 400 degrees for 18 minutes.

Poppy Muffins

$^1/_2$ cup raisins
2 cups oat flour
$^1/_2$ cup whole wheat flour
$2^1/_2$ tsp. baking powder
$^1/_2$ tsp. salt
$^1/_4$ tsp. nutmeg

2 eggs
2 tbsp. oil
4 tbsp. honey or $^1/_4$ cup sugar
1 cup milk
2 tbsp. poppy seeds
2 tsp. lemon peel

Soak raisins for 5 minutes in 1/4 cup boiling water. preheat oven to 350 degrees. Line muffin cups with baking papers. Put oat flour in a bowl, sift in other dry ingredients. Beat together eggs. oil, and honey. Stir milk, raisins and water, poppy seeds, and lemon peel, and add the egg mixture. Add dry to liquid ingredients, stirring just enough to mix well. Spoon into muffin tin and sprinkle with more poppy seeds. Bake until tops are golden brown.

Raisin Date Muffins

1 cup sliced almonds	1 cup vegetable oil
3-4 extra ripe	5 cups flour
bananas, peeled	1 tbsp. baking soda
1 cup cooked	2 tsp. cinnamon
mashed pumpkin	1 tsp. ground cloves
3 eggs	1 cup chopped dates
1½ cups sugar	1 cup raisins

Puree bananas (2 cups). Combine bananas, pumpkin, eggs, and sugar in a bowl. Beat in oil. Combine dry ingredients. Beat into banana mixture. Fold in dates and raisins. Spoon 1/4 cup batter into paper lined muffin tin. Bake muffins at 350 degrees for 25 minutes. Cool. Makes 24 - 30 muffins.

Bananas are a type of berry from a tree classified as an herb tree which can grow up to 30 feet high.

Pumpkin Praline Muffins

2 cup flour
$^2/_3$ cup plus 3 tbsp. brown sugar
2 tsp. baking powder
$^1/_2$ tsp. baking soda
$^1/_2$ tsp.cinnamon
$^1/_4$ tsp. ground nutmeg
$^1/_4$ tsp. ground cloves

$^3/_4$ cup buttermilk
$^1/_3$ cup butter, melted
$^3/_4$ cup pumpkin (canned)
1 egg, beaten
1 tbsp. sour cream
$^1/_3$ cup chopped pecans

In small bowl, stir together 3 tbsp. brown sugar and sour cream. Stir in pecans and set aside.

In medium bowl stir together flour, baking powder, baking soda, cinnamon, nutmeg and cloves.

In another bowl mix eggs, buttermilk, pumpkin, $^2/_3$ cup brown sugar and melted butter. Combine wet ingredients and dry ingredients. Stir just until moist. Fill prepared tins $^2/_3$ full. Spoon 1 tsp. of pecan mixture on top of each muffin. Bake in 400 degree oven for about 20 minutes.

fat-free & low-fat muffins

Standard Substitutions For Fat-Free Muffins

- Use natural applesauce instead of oil (equal exchange) and then double the amount of baking powder used.

- For every egg called for, use two egg whites.

- Use skim milk instead of whole milk.

- When buttermilk is called for, use skim milk and add 1/2 tbsp. lemon juice to skim milk to make fat-free buttermilk.

- Use a fat-free margarine spread to save even more calories.

Lowfat Apple-Cheddar Muffins

1³/₄ cups all-purpose flour
1 cup apples, cored, pared,
   and finely chopped
¹/₂ cup rye flour
¹/₄ cup reduced fat Cheddar
   cheese, shredded
¹/₂ cup chopped walnuts
¹/₄ sugar
2 tbsp. raisins

2 tsp. double-acting
   baking powder
¹/₈ tsp. ground nutmeg
¹/₈ tsp. cinnamon
¹/₂ cup skim milk
¹/₃ cup plus 2 tsp. reduced
   calorie margarine
¹/₄ cup frozen egg
   substitute, thawed

Preheat oven to 375 degrees. In medium mixing bowl combine first ten ingredients; stir to combine and set aside. In blender combine remaining ingredients and process until smooth. Pour into dry ingredients and stir until moistened (do not beat or over mix). Spray nonstick muffin tin with nonstick cooking spray; fill each cup with an equal amount of batter (each will be about 3/4 full). Bake in middle of center oven rack for 20 minutes (until muffins are golden brown and a toothpick inserted in center, comes out dry). Invert muffins onto wire rack and let cool. Yield: 12 muffins

Fat-Free Basic Muffin Mix

Use this as a base for the following recipes

2 cups rolled oats
2 cups whole wheat flour
2 cups all-purpose flour
2 tbsp. baking powder
1 tbsp. cinnamon

1 tsp. nutmeg
1 tbsp. dried orange bits
1 cup skim milk (soured with
$1/2$ tbsp. lemon juice)

Blend oats in food processor until consistency of cornmeal; mix well into other ingredients.

Blueberry Muffins

$2^1/_3$ cups No Fat
  Basic Muffin Mix
1 banana, mashed
1 cup orange juice

1 tsp. vanilla
2 tbsp. canola oil
2 egg whites, beaten
1 cup blueberries

Mix all ingredients together. Spoon batter into prepared muffin tins. Bake at 400 degrees for 20 to 25 minutes. Yield: 10-12 muffins

Apple Muffins

2$\frac{1}{3}$ cups No Fat Basic
    Muffin Mix
1 banana, mashed
$\frac{3}{4}$ cup grated apple
$\frac{1}{4}$ cup raisins
1 cup apple juice

$\frac{1}{4}$ tsp. cinnamon
1 tsp. vanilla extract
2 tbsp. applesauce
2 egg whites, beaten
$\frac{1}{4}$ tsp. baking powder

Mix ingredients together. Spoon batter into prepared muffin tins. Bake at 400 degrees for 20 to 25 minutes. Yield: 10-12 muffins

Fat-Free Bran Muffins

1 cup flour
2 cups bran
$\frac{1}{4}$ cup cornmeal
1 tsp. salt
1$\frac{1}{4}$ cups skim milk

$\frac{1}{2}$ cup molasses
1 tbsp. baking soda,
    dissolved in a little water
1 cup raisins

In large bowl mix all ingredients together. Pour into lined muffin tins. Bake at 325 degrees for 25 minutes.

Fat-Free Carrot Muffins

4 egg whites, beaten	2 tsp. cinnamon
2 cups flour	$1/2$ tsp. salt
$1^1/_2$ cups sugar	1 cup applesauce
2 tsp. baking soda	2 tsp. vanilla extract
1 tbsp. baking powder	2 cups raw carrots, grated

In a medium size bowl beat egg whites; set aside. In a large bowl combine flour, sugar, baking soda, baking powder, cinnamon, and salt. In a separate bowl mix together applesauce, vanilla, and carrots. Pour wet ingredients into dry mixture; stir just until moist. Fold in egg whites and let stand for 20 minutes. Spray muffin tins with a nonfat cooking spray. Fill greased muffin cups 2/3 full. Bake at 350 degrees for approximately 30 minutes or until golden brown.

No Oil Cherry Muffins

3 egg whites, beaten	$1/2$ tsp. salt
1 cup sugar	1 cup chopped nuts
$1^1/_2$ cups flour	1 jar (8 oz.) maraschino cherries,
$1^1/_2$ tsp. baking powder	drained, but save juice

In large bowl beat egg whites; add sugar and beat again. Add cherry juice and stir. Stir in nuts, cherries, flour, salt, and baking powder. Fold in egg whites. Spoon batter into prepared muffin tins. Bake at 350 degrees for about 25 minutes.

Fat-Free Cranberry-Orange Muffins

2 egg whites, beaten
2 cups flour
1 cup sugar
2 tsp. baking powder
$^1/_2$ tsp. baking soda

1 tsp. salt
$^1/_4$ cup applesauce
1 tbsp. orange peel
$^3/_4$ cup orange juice
$1^1/_2$ cups cranberries, chopped

In a medium size bowl beat egg whites; set aside. In a large bowl combine flour, sugar, baking powder, baking soda, and salt. In a separate bowl mix applesauce, orange peel, and orange juice; stir just until moist. Add cranberries to mixture, then fold in egg whites. Spray muffin tins with a non-fat cooking spray. Fill greased muffin cups 2/3 full. Bake at 350 degrees for about 25 to 30 minutes or until golden brown. Yield: 12 muffins

Low-Fat Hodge-Podge Muffins

$1^1/_2$ cups whole wheat flour
$1^1/_2$ cups all-purpose flour
$^3/_4$ cup oatmeal
4 egg whites, beaten
$2^1/_2$ cups applesauce

2 tsp. baking soda
3 tsp. baking powder
3 tsp. cinnamon
1 tsp. nutmeg
$^1/_8$ tsp. allspice

Mix ingredients together in large bowl. Spoon batter into prepared muffin tins. Bake at 350 degrees for 15 to 20 minutes.

Fat-Free Oatmeal Muffins

1$^1/_2$ cups oatmeal
1$^1/_4$ cups flour
$^1/_2$ cup brown sugar
$^3/_4$ tsp. cinnamon
1$^1/_2$ tbsp. baking powder

$^3/_4$ tsp. baking soda
1 cup applesauce
$^1/_2$ cup skim milk
2 egg whites, beaten
$^1/_2$ cup raisins (optional)

Mix ingredients together in large bowl. Spoon batter into prepared muffin tins. Bake at 400 degrees for 18 to 22 minutes.

Fat-Free Poppy Seed Muffins

3 cups flour
1$^1/_2$ cups granulated sugar
1 cup brown sugar
4 egg whites, beaten
3 tsp. baking powder

1$^1/_2$ cups skim milk
1$^1/_2$ cups natural applesauce
1$^1/_2$ tsp. salt
1 tsp. almond extract
2 tbsp. poppy seeds

Mix ingredients together in large bowl. Spoon batter into prepared muffin tins. Bake at 350 degrees for 30 minutes or until golden brown.

Fat-Free Pumpkin Muffins

$3^{1}/_{2}$ cups flour
2 tsp. baking soda
2 tsp. baking powder
$1^{1}/_{2}$ tsp. salt
1 tsp. cinnamon
1 tsp. nutmeg

1 cup applesauce
4 egg whites, beaten
$^{2}/_{3}$ cup water
2 cups canned pumpkin
3 cups sugar

In large bowl beat eggs. Add applesauce, water, sugar, and pumpkin; mix well. Then add flour and spices. Bake at 350 degrees for about 25 to 30 minutes.

Fat-Free Sour Cream Muffins

$^{1}/_{2}$ cup applesauce
1 cup sugar
3 egg whites, beaten
1 cup fat free sour cream
$^{1}/_{4}$ tsp. salt

1 tsp. baking soda
2 tsp. baking powder
2 cups flour
1 tsp. vanilla

Mix ingredients together in large bowl. Spoon batter into prepared muffin tins. Bake at 350 degrees for 15 minutes.

Fat-Free Zucchini Muffins

4 egg whites, beaten   3 cups flour
2 cups sugar   1 tsp. salt
1 cup applesauce   1 tsp. baking soda
2 cups zucchini, grated   1$^1/_2$ tsp. baking powder
2 tsp. vanilla $^1/_4$ cup nuts (optional)

Mix all ingredients together well. Spoon batter into prepared muffin
tins. Bake at 350 degrees for 25 to 30 minutes. Nuts may be added, if
you desire.

Bacon 'n Cheese Muffins

Perfect with a bowl of soup and a tossed salad, and great for breakfast.

1³/₄ cups flour
¹/₃ cup yellow cornmeal
2 tbsp. sugar
2 tsp. baking powder
¹/₄ tsp. salt
¹/₈ tsp. ground red pepper
 (optional)
8 slices bacon, cooked,
 drained, and crumbled

²/₃ cup Cheddar cheese, shredded
1 cup milk
1 egg, lightly beaten
3 tbsp. butter or margarine,
 melted and cooled
¹/₂ tsp. spicy mustard

Preheat oven to 400 degrees. In a large bowl stir together flour, corn-meal, sugar, baking powder, salt, and red pepper; stir in bacon and cheese to coat. In another bowl stir together milk, egg, butter, and mustard until blended. Make a well in center of dry ingredients; add milk mixture and stir just to combine. Spoon batter into prepared muffin tins. Bake 20 to 25 minutes or until a cake tester inserted in center of one muffin comes out clean. Remove muffin tin or tins to wire rack. Cool 5 minutes before removing muffins from cups. Finish cooling on rack. Serve warm or cool completely and store in airtight container in refrigerator. Let muffins reach room temperature or warm slightly before serving. Yield: 10 muffins

German Beer Muffins

3 cups flour
5 tsp. baking powder
$^1/_3$ tsp. salt

3 tbsp. sugar
1 bottle of beer (12 oz.)
$^1/_2$ cup Cheddar cheese, grated

Measure dry ingredients into bowl and pour beer over, stirring to blend. Spoon into greased muffin tin and brush tops with butter. Sprinkle with cheese. Bake at 350 degrees for 15 to 20 minutes.

Cornmeal Chive Muffins

Taste like biscuits!

$1^1/_2$ cups flour
$^1/_2$ cup cornmeal
1 tbsp. baking powder
1 tsp. sugar
$^1/_2$ tsp. salt

$^1/_3$ cup margarine at
    room temperature
3 tbsp. fresh chives, snipped
2 tsp. oregano
$^2/_3$ cup milk

Mix flour, cornmeal, baking powder, sugar, and salt; cut in margarine until mixture resembles coarse meal. Mix in chives and oregano. Add milk and stir with fork until dough forms. Gently knead. Roll dough into balls. Place balls in paper- lined muffin tins. Bake at 425 degrees for 15 minutes.

Berkshire Muffins

$^2/_3$ cup milk
$^1/_2$ cup cornmeal
$^1/_2$ cup cooked rice
$^1/_2$ cup flour
2 tbsp. sugar

3 tsp. baking powder
$^1/_2$ tsp. salt
1 egg, separated; yolk well
    beaten/white beaten stiff
1 tbsp. butter, melted

Preheat oven to 375 degrees. Prepare muffin tins. Scald the milk. Slowly pour the milk on the cornmeal; let stand for 5 minutes. Stir in rice and all dry ingredients. Add the egg yolk and butter; blend well. Gently fold in the egg white. Spoon into muffin cups, filling each about 1/2 full. Bake for about 20 minutes.

Cheese Muffins

2 tbsp. minced chives
2 tbsp. vegetable oil
1 egg
$1^1/_4$ cups buttermilk
$^1/_2$ cup Swiss cheese, grated
$^3/_4$ tsp. dill weed

2 cups rolled oats
$^1/_2$ cup whole wheat flour
$^1/_2$ tsp. salt
$^1/_2$ tsp. baking soda
2 tsp. baking powder

Preheat oven to 375 degrees. Beat the egg, oil, and chives together. Stir in the buttermilk, cheese, and dill weed. Blend the oats in a blender to make 1 1/2 cups of floury meal. Sift the other dry ingredients together, and stir in the oatmeal. Add the dry ingredients to the cheese mixture. Spoon into prepared muffin tins. Bake about 15 minutes or until muffins are a pale, creamy color on top.

Basic Muffin Mix

Mix and keep for quick muffins:

5$^1/_2$ cups flour	$^1/_2$ cup sugar
$^1/_4$ cup baking powder	$^1/_2$ cup butter
1$^1/_2$ tsp. salt	

Mix flour, baking powder, salt, and sugar. Cut in butter until mixture resembles coarse crumbs. Store in a tightly covered container in refrigerator until ready to use.

To make batter combine:

2$^1/_4$ cups Basic Muffin Mix	$^3/_4$ cup plus 1 tbsp. milk
1 egg	

Measure muffin mix into bowl. Beat together egg and milk; add to muffin mix. Stir until moistened. Pour into paper-lined muffin tins. Bake at 425 degrees for 20 to 25 minutes.

HIDDEN CHEESE CENTERS: Fill muffin cups 1/3 full. Place a one-inch cube of cheddar cheese in the center of each. Top with batter.

IRISH MUFFINS: Use 1 cup rye flour and 1 cup white flour. Add 2 tbsp. caraway seeds, and 1/2 cup raisins to batter.

PARMESAN: Sprinkle 1 tbsp. Parmesan cheese over the top of each muffin before baking.

Sausage Corn Muffins

6 small breakfast sausages
3 tbsp. water
1 cup yellow cornmeal
1 cup flour
$^1/_4$ cup sugar
3 tsp. baking powder

$^1/_2$ tsp. salt
1 cup milk
2 eggs
3 tbsp. vegetable oil
$^1/_2$ cup freshly grated
    Parmesan cheese

In a small uncovered skillet cook the sausages in the water over medium-high heat, until the water evaporates and the sausages are browned. Remove from heat and place the sausages on a paper towel to drain. When the sausages are cool enough to handle, chop them up.

Preheat the oven to 425 degrees. Line muffin tins with papers. Combine the cornmeal, flour, sugar, baking powder, and salt in a mixing bowl. Blend thoroughly.

In a separate bowl whisk together the milk, eggs, and vegetable oil. Make a well in the dry ingredients and pour in the egg mixture. Blend with a wooden spoon until a moist lumpy batter is formed. Stir in the cheese and sausage. Spoon into muffin cups. Bake for 20 to 25 minutes. Yield: 12 muffins

Cornmeal, Swiss and Jalapeño Muffins

1$^1/_2$ cups whole wheat flour
$^3/_4$ cup cornmeal
2$^1/_2$ tbsp. sugar
$^3/_4$ tsp. salt
1 tsp. baking powder
1 tsp. baking soda
1 egg, lightly beaten

1 cup sour cream
5 tbsp. milk
1 tbsp. vegetable oil
1 cup Swiss cheese, grated
1 tbsp. finely chopped
  canned jalapeño peppers

Preheat oven to 425 degrees. Place the flour in a large mixing bowl, add the cornmeal, sugar, salt, baking soda, and baking powder. Work the mixture with a fork to eliminate lumps. Add the egg, sour cream, milk and oil, to the dry ingredients. Mix thoroughly. Add the cheese and peppers. Fill muffin cups 2/3 full. Bake for 15 minutes or until golden brown. Yield: 2 1/2 dozen muffins

Ham & Dill Muffins

1³/₄ cups rye flour
¹/₄ cup sugar
2 tsp. baking powder
¹/₂ tsp. salt
1 tsp. dill weed
1 tbsp. caraway seed

1 egg, beaten
³/₄ cup milk
¹/₃ cup vegetable oil
¹/₂ cup Swiss cheese
¹/₂ cup finely
    chopped ham

In a large bowl combine flour, sugar, baking powder, and salt. Make a well in center. In separate bowl combine egg, milk, and oil. Pour egg mixture into well in dry ingredients. Stir just until moist. Batter will be lumpy. Fill paper-lined muffin tins 2/3 full. Bake at 400 degrees for 20 to 25 minutes. Yield: 10-12 muffins

Louisiana Hot Muffins

Great in the morning with eggs

2 cups flour
3 tsp. baking powder
¹/₂ tsp. salt
2 tbsp. sugar
2¹/₄ tsp. cajun seasoning

1 egg
1¹/₄ cup buttermilk
3 tbsp. butter, melted
¹/₂ cup cooked sausage
    (crumbled)

Heat oven to 425 degrees. Mix dry ingredients in large bowl. In smaller bowl mix wet ingredients. Combine and stir just until moistened. Stir in sausage. Fill muffin tins ²/₃ full and bake about 20 minutes.

Hammy Sammy Muffins

1³/₄ cups all-purpose flour
¹/₃ cup rye flour
1 tbsp. packed brown sugar
2 tsp. baking powder
¹/₂ tsp. salt
¹/₂ cup finely chopped
  cooked ham
¹/₂ cup shredded Swiss or
  Cheddar cheese

1 cup milk
¹/₄ cup vegetable oil
1 egg, lightly beaten
1 tsp. prepared spicy
  brown mustard
¹/₄ tsp. Worcestershire sauce
2 drops Tabasco (optional)

Preheat oven to 400 degrees. In a large bowl stir together flours, brown sugar, baking powder, and salt; stir in ham and cheese to coat. In another bowl stir together milk, oil, egg, mustard, Worcestershire, and Tabasco until blended. Make a well in center of dry ingredients; add milk mixture and stir just to combine. Spoon batter into greased muffin tins; bake 20 to 25 minutes or until a cake tester inserted in center of one muffin comes out clean. Remove muffin tins to a wire rack. Cool 5 minutes before removing muffins from cups. Finish cooling on rack. Serve warm or cool completely and store in airtight container in refrigerator. Let muffins reach room temperature or warm slightly before serving. Yield: 10 muffins

Old Fashioned Hot Cross Muffins

An easy-to-make substitute for hot cross buns.

2 cups flour
$^3/_4$ cup sugar
2 tsp. baking powder
$^1/_4$ tsp. salt
$^1/_4$ tsp. cinnamon
$^1/_8$ tsp. ground allspice
1 cup milk

$^1/_2$ cup butter or margarine,
   melted and cooled
1 egg, lightly beaten
1 tsp. vanilla or almond extract
$^1/_4$ tsp. grated orange peel
$^1/_2$ tsp. grated lemon peel
1 cup currants or raisins

Glaze:

$1^1/_2$ tsp. freshly squeezed
   lemon juice

$^1/_3$ cup confectioners sugar

Preheat oven to 375 degrees. In a large bowl stir together flour, sugar, baking powder, salt, cinnamon, and allspice. In a small bowl stir together milk, butter, egg, vanilla, orange peel, and lemon peel. Make a well in center of dry ingredients; add milk mixture and stir just to combine. Stir in currants or raisins. Spoon batter into greased muffin tins; bake 15 to 20 minutes or until a cake tester inserted in center of one muffin comes out clean. Remove muffin tins to wire rack. Cool 5 minutes before removing muffins from cups. Glaze while warm. Finish cooling on rack.

Mexican Muffins

1 cup milk	2 tsp. baking powder
1/4 cup butter, melted	2 tsp. ground cumin
2 eggs, beaten	1/2 tsp. salt
2 cups flour	1/2 cup chopped fresh cilantro

Preheat oven to 400 degrees. Combine milk, butter, and eggs in a medium bowl. Combine flour, baking powder, cumin, and salt in another bowl. Add to milk mixture; stir just until blended. Mix in cilantro. Spoon into paper-lined tins. Bake 15 minutes.

Sour Cream 'n Chive Muffins

3 cups flour	3/4 cup milk
1 tbsp. sugar	1/2 cup sour cream
1 tbsp. baking powder	1/4 cup margarine, melted
1/4 tsp. salt	1/4 cup fresh or freeze-dried
1 egg	chives, chopped

In a large bowl combine flour, sugar, baking powder, and salt. In another bowl whisk egg, milk, sour cream, and margarine. Pour liquid ingredients into dry ingredients; add chives, stirring just until mixed. Spoon batter into greased muffin tins. Bake in preheated 400 degree oven for 20 minutes or until golden brown.

Holiday Mincemeat Muffins

2 cups flour
$^{1}/_{3}$ cup sugar
2 tsp. baking powder
$^{1}/_{4}$ tsp. salt
$1^{1}/_{4}$ cups prepared
   mincemeat

2 eggs, lightly beaten
$^{1}/_{3}$ cup water
$^{1}/_{3}$ cup vegetable oil
1 tsp. vanilla extract
$^{3}/_{4}$ cup chopped walnuts

Preheat oven to 400 degrees. In a large bowl stir together flour, sugar, baking powder, and salt. In another bowl stir together mincemeat, eggs, water, oil, and vanilla until blended. Make a well in center of dry ingredients; add mincemeat mixture and stir just to combine. Stir in walnuts. Spoon batter into greased muffin tins. Bake 20 to 25 minutes or until a cake tester inserted in center of one muffin comes out clean. Remove muffin tins to wire rack. Cool 5 minutes before removing muffins from cups; finish cooling on rack. Serve warm or cool completely and store in an airtight container in refrigerator. Let muffins reach room temperature or warm slightly before serving. These muffins freeze very well. Yield: 12 muffins

Herbed Onion Muffins

$^1/_2$ cup margarine
$^1/_2$ cup chopped
    green onion
2 cups flour
1 tbsp. baking powder

1 tsp. dried thyme
$^1/_2$ tsp. salt
1 egg
1 cup milk

In a small saucepan over medium heat, melt margarine; add green onion. Cook 5 minutes or until tender, stirring occasionally. Meanwhile, in a large bowl combine flour, baking powder, thyme, and salt. In a medium bowl whisk egg and milk; stir in onion. Pour wet ingredients into dry mixture; stir just until moist. Spoon batter into greased muffin tins. Fill cups 2/3 full. Bake at 400 degrees for 20 minutes or until golden brown. Yield: 12 muffins

Fat-Free Potato Muffins

$1^1/_2$ cups flour
2 tbsp. sugar
1 tbsp. baking powder
1 tsp. salt

1 egg white, beaten
$1^1/_2$ cups mashed potatoes
$^2/_3$ cup skim milk

In large bowl mix ingredients together. Spoon batter into prepared muffin tins. Bake at 375 degrees for 30 minutes.

Parmesan, Provolone, and Herb Muffins

2 ¹/₄ cups flour
2 tsp. baking powder
1 tsp. salt
1 tsp. freshly ground
    black pepper
¹/₂ tsp. baking soda
¹/₂ cup freshly grated
    Parmesan cheese
¹/₂ cup grated
    Provolone cheese

¹/₂ cup chopped parsley
1 tsp. dried thyme, crumbled
¹/₂ cup dried savory, crumbled
2 eggs
1 tbsp. vegetable oil
1 tsp. sugar
1¹/₄ cups buttermilk
    or plain yogurt

Preheat oven to 350 degrees. Combine first 5 ingredients in large bowl. Using fork stir in both cheeses and herbs. Whisk eggs, oil, and sugar in another bowl. Mix in buttermilk. Add to dry ingredients; stir to blend. Spoon into paper-lined muffin tins. Bake until a tester comes out clean, approximately 20 minutes.

Pumpernickel Muffins

$^3/_4$ cup rye flour
$^1/_2$ cup all-purpose flour
$^1/_3$ cup firmly packed
    brown sugar
$^1/_4$ cup yellow cornmeal
1 tbsp. unsweetened
    cocoa powder

1 tsp. baking soda
$^1/_4$ tsp. salt
1 cup buttermilk
$^1/_4$ cup butter or margarine,
    melted and cooled
1 egg, lightly beaten
2 tbsp. molasses

Preheat oven to 400 degrees. In a large bowl stir together flours, brown sugar, cornmeal, cocoa, baking soda, and salt. In another bowl stir together buttermilk, butter, egg, and molasses until blended. Make a well in center of dry ingredients; add buttermilk mixture and stir just to combine. Spoon batter into greased muffin tins. Bake 15 to 20 minutes or until a cake tester inserted in center of one muffin comes out clean. Remove muffin tins to a wire rack. Cool 5 minutes before removing muffins from cups; finish cooling on rack. Serve warm or cool completely and store in an airtight container at room temperature. These muffins freeze well. Yield: 9 muffins

Pizza Muffins

Great from freezer to lunch box.

2 cups flour
2 tsp. sugar
2 tsp. baking powder
$1/8$ tsp. oregano
$1/4$ tsp. salt
$1/8$ tsp. ground red
    pepper (optional)
$2/3$ cup Mozzarella
    cheese, shredded

3 tsp. freshly grated
    Parmesan cheese
$1/2$ cup tomato sauce
$1/3$ cup milk
1 egg, lightly beaten
3 tbsp. butter or margarine,
    melted and cooled
$1/3$ cup chopped
    pepperoni or cooked ham

Preheat oven to 400 degrees. In a large bowl stir together flour, sugar, baking powder, oregano, salt, and red pepper; stir in cheese. In another bowl stir together tomato sauce, milk, egg, and butter until blended. Make a well in center of dry ingredients; add tomato sauce mixture and stir just to combine. Stir in pepperoni or ham. Spoon batter into greased muffin tins. Bake 15 to 20 minutes or until a cake tester inserted in center of one muffin comes out clean. Remove muffin tins to wire rack. Cool 5 minutes before removing muffins from cups; finish cooling on rack. Serve warm or cool completely and store in an airtight container in refrigerator. Let muffins reach room temperature or warm slightly before serving. Yield: 9 muffins

made for Dinner 1/6/90

155

Potato 'n Dill Muffins

2 cups flour
1¹/₂ tsp. baking powder
¹/₄ tsp. baking soda
¹/₄ tsp. salt
³/₄ cup milk
¹/₂ cup sour cream
¹/₂ cup mashed,
   cooked potatoes

¹/₄ cup butter or margarine,
   melted and cooled
1 egg, lightly beaten
3 drops Tabasco
3 tsp. finely chopped scallions
¹/₂ tsp. dried dill

Preheat oven to 400 degrees. In a large bowl stir together flour, baking powder, baking soda, and salt. In another bowl stir together milk, sour cream, mashed potatoes, butter, egg, and Tabasco until blended. Make a well in center of dry ingredients; add milk mixture and stir just to combine. Stir in scallions and dill. Batter will be sticky; spoon into greased muffin tins. Bake 15 to 20 minutes or until cake tester inserted in center of one muffin comes out clean. Remove muffin tins to wire rack. Cool 5 minutes before removing muffins from tins; finish cooling on rack. Serve warm or cool completely and store in an airtight container in refrigerator. Let muffins reach room temperature or warm slightly before serving. These muffins freeze well. Yield: 12 muffins

Yellow Squash Muffins

2 cups grated yellow squash
2 tbsp. lemon juice
2 tbsp. maple syrup
2 eggs
1 1/2 cups sifted whole
   wheat pastry flour
1/4 cup wheat germ

2 tsp. baking powder
1/2 tsp. baking soda
1 tsp. cinnamon
1/4 tsp. ginger
1 tbsp. grated lemon rind
3/4 cup chopped walnuts

In a mixing bowl or food processor blend together the squash, lemon juice, maple syrup, and eggs. In another bowl, combine the pastry flour, wheat germ, baking powder, baking soda, cinnamon, ginger, and lemon rind. Preheat oven to 400 degrees. Add the dry ingredients to the squash mixture and process briefly, only until all the flour is moistened. Stir in the walnuts. Spoon the batter into prepared muffin tins. Bake 18 to 20 minutes. Yield: 12 muffins

Sunflower Muffins

1 cup flour
1 cup uncooked rolled oats
$1/2$ cup firmly packed
   brown sugar
$2^1/2$ tsp. baking powder
$1/4$ tsp. salt
$1/2$ cup milk

1 egg, lightly beaten
2 tbsp. butter or margarine,
   melted and cooled
2 tbsp. vegetable oil
1 tsp. vanilla extract
$2/3$ cup sunflower seeds

Preheat oven to 400 degrees. In a large bowl stir together flour, oats, brown sugar, baking powder, and salt. In another bowl stir together milk, egg, butter, oil, and vanilla until blended. Make a well in center of dry ingredients; add milk mixture and stir just to combine. Stir in sunflower seeds. Spoon batter into prepared muffin tins; bake 15 to 20 minutes or until a cake tester inserted in center of one muffin comes out clean. Remove muffin tins to wire rack. Cool 5 minutes before removing muffins from cups; finish cooling on rack. Serve warm or cool completely and store in airtight container at room temperature. These muffins freeze well. Yield: 9 muffins

Swiss Rye Muffins

1 cup all-purpose flour
1 cup rye flour
1½ tsp. baking powder
½ tsp. baking soda
¼ tsp. salt
1⅓ cups shredded
    Swiss cheese
1 cup buttermilk

¼ cup vegetable oil
1 egg, lightly beaten
2 tbsp. molasses
½ tsp. spicy mustard
½ tsp. caraway seeds (optional)
½ tsp. Worcestershire sauce
½ tsp. ground black pepper

Preheat oven to 400 degrees. In a large bowl stir together flours, baking powder, baking soda, and salt. In another bowl stir together buttermilk, oil, egg, molasses, mustard, caraway seeds (if desired), Worcestershire sauce, and pepper until blended. Make a well in center of dry ingredients; add buttermilk mixture and stir just to combine. Spoon batter into prepared muffin tins; bake 15 to 20 minutes or until a cake tester inserted in center of one muffin comes out clean. Remove muffin tins to wire rack. Cool 5 minutes before removing muffins from tins; finish cooling on rack. Serve warm or cool completely and store in airtight container in refrigerator. Let muffins reach room temperature or warm slightly before serving. Yield: 12 muffins

Toasted Sesame Muffins

2 cups flour
2 tsp. baking powder
$^1/_4$ tsp. salt
$^1/_3$ cup sesame seed paste
$^1/_4$ cup butter or margarine,
    melted and cooled
$^1/_2$ tsp. sesame oil

$^3/_4$ cup firmly packed
    brown sugar
$^1/_2$ cup milk
2 eggs, lightly beaten
1 tsp. vanilla
$^1/_3$ cup toasted sesame seeds,
    divided (see note below)

Preheat oven to 400 degrees. In a large bowl stir together flour, baking powder, and salt. In another bowl stir together sesame seed paste, butter, and oil; stir in sugar, milk, eggs, and vanilla until blended. Make a well in center of dry ingredients; add paste mixture and stir just to combine. Stir in half of the sesame seeds. Spoon batter into prepared muffin tins; sprinkle with other half of sesame seeds. Bake 15 to 20 minutes or until a cake tester inserted in center of one muffin comes out clean. Remove muffin tins to wire rack. Cool 5 minutes before removing muffins from tins; finish cooling on rack. Serve warm or cool completely and store in airtight container at room temperature. Yield: 12 muffins

NOTE: To toast sesame seeds, place in small skillet over medium heat. Cook, stirring, for 3 minutes or until seeds are lightly browned.

Sesame seeds are fabulously high in protein.

Sausage 'n Apple Muffins

2 cups flour
1 tbsp. firmly packed
    brown sugar
2$\frac{1}{2}$ tsp. baking powder
$\frac{1}{2}$ tsp. salt
$\frac{1}{4}$ tsp. ground nutmeg
$\frac{3}{4}$ cup shredded Swiss cheese
$\frac{1}{4}$ cup dry white wine

$\frac{1}{3}$ cup vegetable oil
$\frac{1}{2}$ cup water
1 egg, lightly beaten
$\frac{1}{2}$ tsp. spicy brown mustard
$\frac{2}{3}$ pound bulk pork sausage,
    cooked, drained, cooled,
    and crumbled
$\frac{3}{4}$ cup diced apple

Preheat oven to 375 degrees. In a large bowl stir together flour, brown sugar, baking powder, salt, and nutmeg. Stir in cheese to coat. In another bowl stir together wine, oil, water, egg, and mustard. Make a well in center of dry ingredients; add wine mixture and stir just to combine. Stir in sausage and apple. Spoon batter into greased muffin tins. Bake 15 to 20 minutes or until a cake tester inserted in center of one muffin comes out clean. Remove muffin tins to wire rack. Cool 5 minutes before removing muffins from tins; finish cooling on rack. Serve warm or cool completely and store in airtight container in refrigerator. Let muffins reach room temperature or warm slightly before serving. Yield: 12 muffins

Apples are capable of lasting 3-5 weeks in the refrigerator and will retain vitamin C content.

Tomato Basil Cornmeal Muffins

1 cup cornmeal
1 can (14 oz.) tomatoes,
   including liquid
2 eggs
3 tbsp. brown sugar
$^1/_2$ cup vegetable oil
$^1/_2$ tsp. dried sweet basil,
   or to taste

$1^1/_2$ cups flour
1 tbsp. baking powder
$^1/_2$ tsp. baking soda
$^1/_2$ tsp. salt
$^1/_4$ tsp. garlic powder

In small bowl combine cornmeal and canned tomatoes; let soak for 15 minutes. In a large bowl combine eggs, brown sugar, and oil; mix well. Add prepared cornmeal mixture and basil; stir well. In another bowl combine flour, baking powder, baking soda, salt, and garlic powder. Add dry ingredients to wet mixture and fold together gently just until mixed. Spoon batter into prepared muffin tins. Bake at 400 degrees for 25 minutes. Yield: 12 muffins

CORNMEAL WITH TOMATO BITS: Substitute 1 1/4 cups milk for canned tomatoes. Reduce oil to 1/4 cup and add 1 cup peeled, seeded, and chopped fresh tomatoes to wet mixture.

Basil comes from a plant belonging to the mint family native to India and Iran.

Zucchini Rice Muffins

$^1/_2$ cup chopped raisins
1 cup hot water
1$^1/_4$ cups brown rice flour
    (whole wheat flour may
    be substituted)
1 cup whole wheat flour
2 tbsp. powdered milk
1 tbsp. baking powder
$^3/_4$ tsp. salt

$^1/_2$ tsp. ground ginger
$^1/_2$ cup oat bran
3 tbsp. honey
3 tbsp. vegetable oil
1 egg
1 tsp. grated lemon peel
1$^1/_2$ cups grated zucchini
$^3/_4$ cup of the raisin water

Preheat oven to 375 degrees. Line muffin tins with paper. Soak the raisins in the hot water. In mixing bowl sift the dry ingredients together, adding the bran after mixing. In another bowl cream the honey and oil together; add the egg and lemon peel. Strain the raisins and measure the soaking water. Add or discard water to make 3/4 cup. Mix with the grated zucchini and raisins. Stir the flour and the zucchini mixture alternately into the egg mixture. Spoon batter into muffin tins. Bake for 15 to 20 minutes. (This is a very moist muffin. The testing knife will look a little wet, but it should not be gooey.)

Honey should be stored at room temperature to keep it from crystallizing.

Piping hot tips for making perfect muffins

Read all of the directions before starting.

Make sure the oven is fully preheated to the required temperature.

Bake on the center rack to avoid burning on top or bottom.

Select the freshest ingredients available. Fresh herbs make a tremendous difference in savory muffin recipes.

For all recipes (unless otherwise noted), use this technique: Mix all the wet ingredients together; to save on dishes, I mix them together right in a big glass measuring cup. Stir dry ingredients together and form a well in the center of the bowl. Pour the wet ingredients into the well and lightly fold together.

The biggest mistake people make is over-stirring. This makes muffins too dense. To achieve the result of light and airy muffins, stir just until all of the ingredients are moist.

Muffin liners can give you mixed results; for consistent results, use a no-stick cooking spray.

Fill each muffin tin $^3/_4$ way full. If you don't have enough batter to fill all the cups in a muffin tin, carefully put water in the empty cups; this promotes even cooking.

Muffins are done when they're golden brown on top. Muffins can easily overbake in a dark muffin tin so reduce the oven temperature by 25 degrees.

Sift flour or buy pre-sifted flour for best results unless otherwise noted.

Unless the recipe says otherwise, immediately remove muffins from the pan after taking them out of the oven. The reason: muffins will become soggy from the steam trapped between the muffin and the muffin cup. The exception to this is fruit muffins, which need a few minutes to settle.

How to make mini-muffins and jumbo muffins

These are easy to make; the only special equipment you need are mini-muffin tins and jumbo muffin tins. There's no need to adapt the recipe or the oven temperature. A regular recipe for 12 regular muffins will make two dozen mini-muffins or six jumbo muffins. Mini-muffins take about five minutes less to bake than regular muffins; jumbo muffins take about five minutes more.

Fruit, nut and chocolate muffins make wonderful jumbo muffins, but not mini-muffins because the fruit chunks, etc. are too large to fit in the tiny cups.

Weights and Measures

Dash = less than $1/8$ tsp.

$1/2$ tbsp. = $1\,1/2$ tsp.

1 tbsp. = 3 tsp.

2 tbsp. = $1/8$ cup

$1/4$ cup = 4 tbsp.

$1/3$ cup = 5 tbsp. plus 1 tsp.

$1/2$ cup = 8 tbsp.

$3/4$ cup = 12 tbsp.

1 cup = 16 tbsp.

$1/2$ pint = 1 cup or 8 fluid ounces

1 pint = 2 cups or 16 fluid ounces

1 quart = 4 cups or 2 pints or 32 fluid ounces

1 gallon = 16 cups or 4 quarts

1 pound = 16 ounces

Substitutions

If you don't have:

Use:

1 tsp. baking powder

$^1/_4$ tsp. baking soda plus $^1/_2$ tsp. cream of tartar

$^1/_2$ cup firmly packed brown sugar

$^1/_2$ cup granulated sugar mixed with 2 tbsp. molasses

1 cup buttermilk

1 tbsp. lemon juice or vinegar plus milk to equal 1 cup (Stir; let mixture stand for 5 minutes.)

1 oz. (1 square) unsweetened baking chocolate

3 tbsp. unsweetened cocoa plus 1 tbsp. shortening

3 oz. (3 squares) semi-sweet baking chocolate

3 oz. ($^1/_2$ cup) semi-sweet chocolate chips

$^1/_2$ cup corn syrup

$^1/_2$ cup granulated sugar plus 2 tbsp. liquid

1 whole egg

2 egg yolks plus 1 tbsp. water

1 cup honey

$1^1/_4$ cups granulated sugar plus $^1/_4$ cup water

1 tsp. freshly grated orange or lemon peel

$^1/_2$ tsp. dried peel

1 tsp. pumpkin pie spice

$^1/_2$ tsp. cinnamon, $^1/_4$ tsp. nutmeg and $^1/_8$ tsp. each allspice and cardamom

When substituting cornstarch or arrowroot for flour as a thickener, use only half as much.

Equivalents

Almonds, blanched, slivered	4 oz. = 1 cup
Apples	1 medium = 1 cup sliced
Bananas	1 medium, mashed = $1/3$ cup
Butter or margarine	2 cups = 1 lb. or 4 sticks 1 cup = $1/2$ lb. or 2 sticks $1/2$ cup = 1 stick or 8 tbsp. $1/4$ cup = $1/2$ stick or 4 tbsp.
Chocolate	1 (6-oz.) pkg. chocolate chips= 1 cup chips or 6 (1 oz.) squares semisweet chocolate
Cocoa, unsweetened	1 (8-oz.) can = 2 cups
Coconut, flaked	$3^1/2$ oz. = $1^1/3$ cups
Cream cheese	3-oz. package = 6 tbsp. 8-oz. package = 1 cup
Flour White or all-purpose Whole Wheat	 1 lb. = $3^1/2$ to 4 cups 1 lb. = $3^3/4$ to 4 cups
Honey, liquid	16 oz. = $1^1/3$ cups
Lemons	1 medium = 1 to 3 tbsp. juice and 2 to 3 tsp. grated peel

Milk
Evaporated   5-oz. can = $^5/_8$ cup
                                             12-oz. can = $1^1/_2$ cups
Sweetened, condensed   14-oz. can = $1^1/_4$ cups

Oranges   1 medium = 6 to 8 tbsp.
                                             juice and 2 to 3 tsp. grated peel

Pecans, shelled   1 lb. = 4 cups halved,
                                             $3^1/_2$ to 4 cups chopped

Raisins, seedless, whole   1 lb. = $2^3/_4$ to 3 cups

Shortening   1 lb. = $2^1/_2$ cups

Sugar
Granulated   1 lb. = $2^1/_2$ cups
Brown, packed   1 lb. = $2^1/_4$ cups
Confectioners' or powdered   1 lb. = $3^3/_4$ to 4 cups, unsifted

Walnuts, chopped $4^1/_2$ oz. = 1 cup

Index

Additional Information

Consider giving a copy of Marilyn Taylor's
Muffin Madness to a busy mom or your favorite baker.

It's a perfect stocking stuffer or just a delicious way to say "I love you."
For only $12.95 (plus $3.50 for shipping and handling), it will warm up
a kitchen and more than a few hearts. Order your copy today!

Rhodes & Easton
121 E. Front St., 4th Floor
Traverse City, MI 49684
1-800-706-4636

MUFFIN MADNESS

Cover design by Barbara Hodge

*Text design by Barbara Hodge in Adobe Garamond
with display lines in Bodega Sans Black*

Text stock is 60 lb. Avenor Artica

*Printed and bound by Data Reproductions
Rochester Hills, Michigan*

Production Editor: Alex Moore